EVOLVING
GOD-IMAGES

EVOLVING GOD-IMAGES

ESSAYS ON RELIGION, INDIVIDUATION,
AND POSTMODERN SPIRITUALITY

Edited by Patrick J. Mahaffey, PhD

iUniverse LLC
Bloomington

EVOLVING GOD-IMAGES
Essays on Religion, Individuation, and Postmodern Spirituality

iUniverse books may be ordered through booksellers or by contacting:

iUniverse LLC
1663 Liberty Drive
Bloomington, IN 47403
www.iuniverse.com
1-800-Authors (1-800-288-4677)

ISBN: 978-1-4917-3244-1 (sc)
ISBN: 978-1-4917-3411-7 (hc)
ISBN: 978-1-4917-3243-4 (e)

Library of Congress Control Number: 2014909233

Printed in the United States of America.

iUniverse rev. date: 05/28/2014

Front cover image © is from an original painting by Rebecca Gomez
www.rgomezart.com

For my students

CONTENTS

Part I
Theistic and Monistic Spirituality

Part IV
Atheist and Secular Spirituality

FOREWORD

The essays gathered together in this volume represent a deeply moving example of what can happen in a classroom when, almost magically, the professor's wisdom and enthusiasm, the archetypal power of the subject-matter itself, and the openness of the students converge.

In the spring of 2013 for the first time Dr. Patrick Mahaffey taught a graduate seminar on "The God Complex" to a third year group of students in our Mythological Studies Program at Pacifica Graduate Institute. He was so stirred by the reflection papers the students wrote that he decided to set aside work on a manuscript of his own to put together this collection of essays, along with his own account of the themes explored in the course. The result beautifully communicates his loving appreciation of the diversity, honesty, and maturity of his students.

I do believe it's pertinent that this was a new course for Patrick. There is always something special about the first time we teach a particular class. You might expect that we would be at our very best the following year, after we'd had an opportunity to learn from what didn't quite work that first time around and are still very much creatively working on putting our syllabus together—but there will never again be quite that special blend of excitement, apprehension, and wonder that we bring to a course when it is as new for us as it is for our students—something that I believe somehow makes it a more fully joint exploration than ever quite happens again.

As the title of the volume, *Evolving God-Images: Essays on Religion, Individuation, and Postmodern Spirituality,* indicates, the course focused on religion and spirituality. The students were encouraged to consider their understanding, their own *experience,* of this aspect of their lives. The papers gathered here make clear how much they welcomed the invitation to reflect on their own relationship to God, the divine, the numinous. In a sense they may have, mostly unconsciously perhaps, been waiting for such an opportunity. Earlier that same year they had participated in classes on religious approaches to mythology, on Hebrew and Jewish traditions, on Islam, and on Christianity. I imagine this may well have left them with a readiness to explore "where does all this leave *me?*"

Reading these papers reminded me how rare it is in our culture to talk explicitly with one another about our religious beliefs and experiences. On my only visit to India I remember being struck by how freely in the midst of even the most casual encounters, such as sitting across from one another in a railway carriage, Indians would ask me how much money I made, whether I enjoyed sex, and whether I believed in God— all questions that seem to be almost taboo here. Somehow Patrick created a context where sharing about the third of these in often very personal ways seemed natural.

The volume begins with an indication of Patrick's own contribution to the seminar, as he discusses the primary perspectives on religion put forward in the assigned readings: Mark C. Taylor's sophisticated analysis of the persistence of religion in a post-theistic secular world; Carl Jung's focus on our *experiences* of the divine, on the God-images that emerge spontaneously in our psyches, and on how the journey toward wholeness, toward what he called "individuation," can serve as a religious path for those who have broken free from traditional religions; Marion Woodman's revalorization of the divine feminine; the Dalai Lama's conviction that what is at the core of our humanity, irrespective of what religion we adhere to, indeed irrespective of whether we are religious or not, is compassion.

This part of the book led me to reflect on my own response to these perspectives. I found myself grateful for how clearly Mark C. Taylor distinguishes the dogmatically anti-religion polemics of the "New Atheists" from the kind of non-theism that seems close to how I'd describe my own spirituality. But what I found most compelling was (as my italics above intimate) the emphasis on experience as over against intellectual apprehension, put forward most emphatically in Jung's affirmation: "I don't have to believe, I *know.*" This helped me realize that what has probably been most important in keeping me connected to the Quakerism in which I grew up was George Fox's central claim: "And this I knew *experimentally.*" Yet, when in his discussion of Jung Patrick seems to be identifying with those for whom "neither sin and redemption, nor ignorance and wisdom, but rather fragmentation and wholeness form the center of the religious quest," I find myself demurring. I turn instead to James Hillman for whom (as I read him) the acceptance of fragmentation rather than the search for wholeness represents spiritual maturity and to Sigmund Freud for whom the central challenge is not the move from ego to Self but that from narcissism to Eros.

But of course it's not my response, but rather that of the students that gives this book its life. Although not all of the essays directly engage the assigned texts, all of them communicate that what happened in class had a real impact. And indeed some do primarily focus on one or more of the readings, sometimes primarily to rehearse their arguments or to critique them, sometimes to use them as a springboard for exploring their own experience. (I couldn't help but enjoy one student's acknowledgement that "Taylor is brilliant but I blow glass" and another's acknowledgement that, though he envies Taylor's academic achievements, "I am glad I don't write like him.")

I need to confess that those essays that focused on or took off from personal anecdotes were the ones that spoke most powerfully to me. This might be in part because I know these students, I have taught them in each of the three years they have been at Pacifica, so of course I was taken by these accounts of some of their most formative experiences—yet I believe other readers will be equally moved.

It was striking to me how warmly many spoke of early childhood immersion in traditional religious communities that they no longer feel connected to intellectually but which nevertheless they know to be part of who they are. Others, also referring to very early powerful childhood experiences of the divine, focus instead on early recognitions of a difference, as one put it, between "my God" and "church God," that sustained them through difficult childhoods and continues to do so. In contrast, another wrote, at the age of seven, about having a beautiful vision of God as a "big ball of golden light providing warmth, love, and safety" that was shattered when just a year later she learned of the Holocaust.

Others acknowledge a continued attachment to the religions of their forefathers and foremothers in ways they feel to be new, creative, life giving. Several articulate why theism, belief in a transcendent God, still pulls them: it provides us with an assurance that our deep longing to know that we are loved is fulfilled; it assures us that we are not alone.

Many speak of *not* knowing how they understand or would name the divine and of being comfortable with that. This to me suggests a new kind of agnosticism for which not knowing is not a preliminary place one hopes to get past, but somehow a deeper truth. Thus, one student speaks of how in meditation the questions and answers about God have come to seem superfluous. Another writes, "I don't know if I ever found God, but I found the warmth of silence."

As someone for whom a relationship with the energies represented by the Greek goddesses has been life shaping, I felt particularly close to those among the women who wrote of how important feminist spirituality, the divine feminine, or goddesses have been to them. Two, very movingly, write of how central their experiences of pregnancy, childbirth, and mothering are to their understanding of the divine. As one put it, "In my baby's eyes I see the face of God."

Several of these students are artists and for them it seems to be their art that most deeply connects them to the divine. One remembers how her first painting, when she was only five years old, was of her image of God (though she was too embarrassed to let others know what it was!). My art, says another, provides me with "a place from which to face the unknown." "Art brings the hidden into view," says yet another, and still another writes of "reveling in the colors of God." This student saw those colors in his art, but others speak of seeing them in the natural world, for instance in "sunlight filtering through the leaves of a mulberry tree" or they see the divine in other aspects of the world as it shows itself to us, in "a violent thunderstorm or the call of an owl in the lonely hours of the night."

Among the many different words used in these essays to point to the essence of the divine are *warmth, silence, balance, harmony,* and again and again, *love,* "the heart's realm of intertwined, interdependent relationship." But there is little sentimental in this emphasis on love; it is accompanied by a profound recognition of the tragic side of life, the inescapability of death and suffering, of underworld experience. Several spoke of how profoundly their understanding of god had been shaken, deepened and transformed by the Holocaust. As one put it, "God is love—and God is death."

I hope I have communicated the rich diversity among these students' perspectives. Some of this no doubt derives from their very different family backgrounds and biographical experience, some perhaps (as several of the essayists themselves suggest) from the kind of given temperamental differences Jung tries to distinguish through his typology—but mostly I think this diversity is not really to be explained or interpreted so much as to be celebrated.

Toward the end of his own contribution to this volume, Patrick writes about the Dalai Lama's recognition that the perspectives of the various world religions do not in fact ultimately converge, and that their ineluctable differences provide us with the challenge of truly honoring the other *as other.* My sense is that this applies beautifully to the interaction among the essays in this marvelous book: implicitly each speaks to the others with "a genuine recognition and respect for the others' reality."

Dr. Christine Downing, Professor
Mythological Studies Program
Pacifica Graduate Institute

ACKNOWLEDGEMENTS

The publication of this book occurs during the twentieth anniversary year of the Mythological Studies Program at Pacifica Graduate Institute. I am grateful to my colleagues for their collaboration in developing the only doctoral program in mythology in the country. Each of the core faculty members is an inspiring teacher and an exemplary scholar: Professors Christine Downing, Laura Grillo, Ginette Paris, Glen Slater, Dennis Slattery, Evans Lansing Smith, and the late V. Walter Odajnyk. I wish to express special thanks to Christine Downing for her Foreword. I want to acknowledge Glen Slater for coining "The God Complex" as a title for the seminar that generated the essays for this volume. Rebecca Gomez generously allowed me to use one of her splendid paintings for the book cover. My appreciation extends to Dr. Stephen Aizenstat, Dr. Patricia Katsky, and Meghan Saxton Sandoval, for their steadfast support of the Mythological Studies Program. I also offer my heartfelt gratitude to my wife, Nina Mahaffey, for her editing assistance and loving support.

PREFACE

More than a century ago, Friedrich Nietzsche proclaimed the death of God as a defining characteristic of the modern world. Today we live in a secularized world shaped largely by science and technology. Religion, nevertheless, continues to have a pervasive influence in the postmodern world of the twenty-first century. Secularization, however, has turned out to be less inevitable and irreversible than expected. Since the 1970s, there has been a dramatic resurgence of religion, including but by no means limited to the rise of fundamentalism. Our times are also distinguished by an unprecedented degree of pluralism. We are awash in a plethora of worldviews—secular and religious. While no single narrative can convincingly explain the complexities of human culture and the natural world, it is imperative that we strive to understand perspectives and values that differ from our own, particularly the world's diverse religious traditions. The future of humanity—even of the planet—depends upon it. As His Holiness the Dalai Lama observes, "The challenge of peaceful co-existence will define the task of humanity in the twenty-first century" (*Toward a True Kinship of Faiths* x). Understanding diverse and conflicting worldviews requires that we examine our attitudes regarding religion, secularity, nature, and the purpose of human existence.

The reflective essays in this volume express the results of such an investigation undertaken in the context of a seminar, entitled "The God Complex," taught within an interdisciplinary doctoral program devoted to the study of myth, religious traditions, depth psychology, and culture. According to C. G. Jung, complexes are *feeling-toned ideas* that accumulate around certain archetypes such as *mother* and *father*. When complexes are constellated or activated, they are inevitably accompanied by emotions and are relatively autonomous. *God*, too, may be construed as an archetype, and the term typically arouses a complex, or emotional charge, in each of us, whether positive or negative.

The introduction to the book provides a discussion of three theoretical topics investigated in the seminar. The first, informed by Mark C. Taylor's theory of religion and his analysis of the emerging network culture of the twenty-first century, concerns the implications of the death of God in Western modernity. The issues addressed include contrary tendencies in contemporary life: secularization versus fundamentalism; transcendent and immanent conceptions of the divine; and monistic and dualistic perspectives on reality. Taylor's own proposal for a religion without God and an ethics without absolutes is a creative response to the challenge of living in a complex and uncertain world. C. G. Jung's concepts of the God-image and individuation comprise the second topic of inquiry. His psychology is presented as a form of postmodern spirituality. Attention is given to the epistemological basis of Jung's psychology and the primacy he accords direct experience as opposed to doctrine. Jung's own life serves as an example of individuation—the need to find one's own way—and as a path to wholeness. His theory of the evolution of the God-image in the history of the West is discussed. Also central to this discussion are Marion Woodman's quest to retrieve the divine feminine and her vision of a God-image that integrates masculine and feminine principles. This path embraces the wisdom in nature and the body as a locus of spirit. The final topic explores the implications of religious pluralism for postmodern spirituality. The life and work of His Holiness the Dalai Lama are presented as an exemplary contribution to achieving both a world of peaceful coexistence and a secular ethics that can be embraced by both religious and secular persons.

The subsequent chapters of the book consist of essays that exemplify different God-images and modes of spirituality. They cluster into four categories: (1) theistic and monistic spirituality; (2) the divine feminine and goddess spirituality; (3) Eastern and contemplative spirituality; and (4) atheist and secular spirituality. Many of the contributions could be appropriately placed in more than one of these categories with respect to theoretical and thematic issues. Theoretical issues include different attitudes regarding the interpretation of religion and the manner and/or degree to which depth psychology is utilized to articulate one's self-understanding. Prominent themes that recur in many of the essays concern whether the divine is conceptualized as immanent, transcendent or both; attitudes toward nature and the body; the impact of religion on gender and God-images; ethnic and cultural heritage; existential issues such as childbirth and motherhood, illness and death; and the impact of trauma in one's life. The contributors include sixteen women and eight men from a variety of cultural backgrounds. While most of the essayists are in their forties, the youngest are in their late twenties and the oldest are in their sixties or early seventies. Accordingly, the essays reflect a wide range of life experiences and diverse professional backgrounds in fields such as art, education, business, healthcare, psychotherapy, and religious education.

Introduction

Patrick J. Mahaffey

> If you are boys, your God is a woman. If you are women, your God is a boy. If you are men, your God is a maiden. The God is where you are not . . . . So: if you are childlike beings now, your God will descend from the height of ripeness to age and death. But if you are developed beings, having engendered or given birth, in body or in soul, so your God rises from the radiant cradle, to the incalculable height of the future, to the maturity and fullness of the coming time. He who still has his life before him is a child. He who lives in the present is developed. If you thus live all that you can live, you are developed. He who is a child in this time, his God dies. He who is developed in this time, his God continues to live. The spirit of the depths teaches this mystery.
>
> —C. G. Jung, *The Red Book: Liber Novus*

A careful investigation of God-images requires contextualization. I begin with a discussion of some of the historical implications of the death of God in the modern West through an examination of some contrary tendencies in contemporary culture. In the second section, attention is given to C. G. Jung's concepts of the God-image and individuation; also addressed is Marion Woodman's effort to retrieve the divine feminine through a quest for wholeness that restores balance between the masculine and feminine principles. The final section explores how religious pluralism can engender a postmodern spirituality and an ethical principle that is responsive to the pressing challenges of the twenty-first century.

1

The Death of God in Western Modernity

The rise of modernity in the West is associated with the rise of science, industrial capitalism, and the decline of traditional religious authority. By the end of the nineteenth century, some of the most influential philosophers and writers of the day no longer saw the once comforting absolutes of European culture as viable. The age of relativism and a sense of meaninglessness had dawned. The impact of modernity on religion was famously proclaimed in Friedrich Nietzsche's *The Gay Science*:

> Have you not heard of that madman who lit a lantern in the bright morning hours, ran to the market place, and cried incessantly, "I seek God! I seek God!" . . . "Whither is God?" he cried. "I shall tell you. We have killed him—you and I. All of us are his murderers. But how have we done this? How were we able to drink the sea? Who gave us the sponge to wipe away the entire horizon? What did we do when we unchained this earth from its sun? . . . Do we not smell anything yet of God's decomposition? Gods too decompose. God is dead. God remains dead. And we have killed him" (Nietzsche 95-96).

For Nietzsche, the basic assumptions of art, philosophy, science, and religion were without any ultimate foundation. If there are no absolutes, then the products of human culture, including religions, are little more than useful fictions, constructed realities that serve particular social functions and address deeply felt personal needs for security and certainty.

Religion

In *After God*, Mark C. Taylor provides a far-ranging discussion of the impact of the Protestant Reformation on modernity and postmodernity. He offers a definition of religion that underscores its pervasive influence in culture: "*Religion is an emergent, complex, adaptive network of symbols, myths, and rituals that, on the one hand, figure schemata of feeling, thinking, and acting in ways that lend life meaning and purpose and, on the other, disrupt, dislocate, and disfigure every stabilizing structure"* (12; italics added). Taylor's definition helps account for the fact that religions can be the source of a viable, adaptive worldview for some individuals and groups or, alternatively, rigidify into fundamentalist forms of belief and practice for persons who resist the myriad changes in the social, economic, and political conditions of contemporary life. He also offers insights regarding three contrary tendencies that animate the dynamic interplay between religion and Western culture: secularization versus fundamentalism; transcendent versus immanent conceptions of the divine; and dualistic versus monistic perspectives on reality.

Secularization versus Fundamentalism

Secularization has been a key concept in the sociology of religion and is closely related to the concept of modernity and the reactions it provokes, such as fundamentalism. A linear conception of historical development concerning religion has dominated Western thought. Social science, born in nineteenth century evolutionism, presupposed this notion and has contributed many of the master terms used in contemporary discourse about social change: industrialization, modernization, rationalization, and urbanization. All of these terms imply one-directional processes and, taken together, constitute the basis for the secularization thesis: the idea that society moves away from some sacred condition to successively secular conditions in which the sacred evermore recedes (Hammond 1). The resurgence of religion during the past three decades, including fundamentalisms, belies this thesis and requires a theory of religion that can account for this dramatic change. As Taylor observes:

> You cannot understand the world today if you do not understand religion. Never before has religion been so powerful and so dangerous. No longer confined to church, synagogue, and mosque, religion has taken to the street by filling airways and networks with images and messages that create fatal conflicts, which threaten to rage out of control. When I began pondering these issues in the 1960s, few analysts

or critics would have predicted this unexpected turn of events. (xiii)

The relationship between religion and secularization has been misunderstood. Taylor further asserts:

> All too often critics did not appreciate the intricate relation between secularity and the Western religious and theological tradition . . . . Religion and secularity are not opposites; to the contrary, Western secularity is a *religious* phenomenon . . . . Secularists misinterpret religion as much as believers misunderstand secularism. Religion is not a separate domain but pervades all culture and has an important impact on every aspect of society. (xiii)

He offers an alternative to the either/or perspective or binary thinking that has served as the conventional wisdom for understanding religion and its secular and atheistic critics. Indeed, one of the most pressing dangers we currently face is the conflict between competing absolutisms that divide the world, oppositions that Taylor argues can never be mediated. Taylor promotes a relational worldview as a creative alternative to this impasse. "In a world where to be is to be connected, absolutism must give way to relationalism, in which everything is codependent and coevolves" (xvii).

Christian fundamentalism arose from American millennial sects of the nineteenth century and came to be associated with a reaction to social and political liberalism and the theory of evolution. We now recognize that all of the major religious traditions contain some fundamentalist elements such as literalist interpretations of scripture and reactivity to aspects of modernity and secular culture. Taylor describes this phenomenon as a worldwide rise in neofoundationalism. He understands this development as a symptom and response to the process of globalization. In his view, while modernism is correlative with industrialization, postmodernism is inseparable from the emergence of postindustrial *network culture* (3). Network culture creates a world in which *to be is to be connected*. However, as connectivity spreads, complexity increases and instability and uncertainty grow. These developments, Taylor observes, lead to a longing for simplicity, certainty, and security. Neofoundationalism, in all of its guises, represents an effort to satisfy this desire: it takes a surprising variety of forms, ranging from the scriptural literalism of Christian evangelicals and some Islamists to the genomic logocentrism and neurophysiological reductionism of some of today's most sophisticated scientists. These disparate forms of belief are alternative versions of a religiosity that attempts to banish doubt by absolutizing relative norms and by dividing the world into exclusive opposites like good/evil, sacred/profane, religious/secular, Western/Eastern, white/black, and Christian/Muslim (4).

Transcendent versus Immanent Conceptions of the Divine

Since the time of the Protestant Reformation, Christian theology has alternated between an emphasis on the transcendent and immanent conceptions of the divine. With the rise of science, the philosophers of the European Enlightenment and Romanticism shifted theology's focus to the immanence of the divine inherent in the natural world. Modern theology began with Friedrich Schleiermacher's publication of *On Religion: Speeches to its Cultured Despisers* in 1799, a work that remains the definitive Romantic interpretation of religion. Schleiermacher's God is immanent in the cosmos; every finite thing is a sign of the infinite (187-88). Protestant liberals subsequently reinterpreted Martin Luther's view of the Kingdom of God in ethical terms, calling for the transformation of social, political, and economic structures. History became the stage for humankind's gradual progress toward a just and equitable society (189-91). This vision of progress became less compelling during World War I. The horrors of war-ravaged Europe made the liberal belief in both the immanence of God and the arrival of the kingdom of God on earth seem little more than a cruel joke. In this context, Karl Barth rejected the pretensions of theological liberalisms by asserting that God is "Wholly Other" and qualitatively different from humanity. His theology, through its emphasis on divine transcendence, became known as neoorthodoxy (191-92).

In the 1960s the pendulum swung back towards immanence. The distance between God and humanity alienated believers living in an increasingly secular society. The death of God theologians, such as Thomas Altizer, critiqued the distant God-image of neoorthodoxy and reasserted the immanence of the divine. Taylor summarizes the reversal entailed by this radical mode of religious thought:

> In Thomas Altizer's dialectical vision, "true" theology is inescapably atheistic. God, however, does not simply disappear; rather, a particular notion of God—more specifically, neoorthodoxy's wholly other God—dies in an act of self-emptying that issues in a realized eschatology that totally transforms the present. Borrowing Nietzsche's description of the moral God, who is the negation of the religious vision of Jesus, Altizer argues that the distant God of neoorthodoxy is "the contradiction of life, instead of being its transfiguration and eternal Yes! This Wholly Other is the God of Hegel's unhappy consciousness and Nietzsche's devoted Christian. Since this God is always elsewhere, believers can approach the divine only by withdrawing from the world as we know it. (200-201).

In denying the neoorthodox God-image, Altizer rejects all the oppositions that such transcendence engenders. In this way, the death of this otherworldly God becomes a worldly faith that deems the secular sacred and the sacred secular (201). Such a reversal is a vision of total presence or immanence; it is, to use the title of one of Alitzer's books, the gospel of Christian atheism (136, 154-57).

The death of God theology, however, failed to anticipate the resurgence of religion that soon followed in the 1970s and that persists into the twenty-first century. The reason, Taylor observes, was that neoorthodoxy and the death of God theology were mirror images of each other and mistaken in opposite ways. The former view entails a commitment to an exclusive and dualistic logic of either/or that obscures the codependence and coevolution of opposites, whereas the latter mode of thought is preoccupied with identity and presence, a monistic view that represses the differences without which nothing can be what it is. Neither monism nor dualism, in Taylor's view, are adequate if we are to comprehend the complexities of emerging network culture (205).

Monistic versus Dualistic Perspectives on Reality

God-images, whether positive or negative, are aspects of our worldview or perspective on reality. Such images express our ultimate existential concerns and reflect our temperament or psychological typology. Taylor describes such perspectives as *schemas* which denote the models or theories by which persons understand the real; I use the term *worldview* as an equivalent term in this essay to describe distinctive attitudes and visions of life. In Taylor's view, every religious schema must provide a way to figure or represent the real: here or elsewhere, inside or outside, above or below (37). He discusses monism and dualism as contrary schemas and correlates them with the two basic varieties of religious experience delineated by William James in his classic *Varieties of Religious Experience*: the religion of healthy-mindedness (monism) and the sick soul (dualism). The healthy-minded are optimistic and at home in the world. As James explains:

> In many persons happiness is congenital and irreclaimable. "Cosmic emotion" inevitably takes in them the form of enthusiasm and freedom. I speak not only of those who are animally happy. I mean those who, when unhappiness is offered or proposed to them, positively refuse to feel it, as if it were something mean and wrong. We find such persons in every age, passionately flinging themselves upon their sense of the goodness of life, in spite of hardships of their own condition, and in spite of the sinister theologies into which they may be born. From the outset their religion is one of union with the divine. (79)

This type of religion entails the conviction that there is an original union or identity between the self and God, an identity that persists throughout life. Evil and corruption are epiphenomenal. For James, the best examples of this attitude are the romantic poets and philosophical idealists like Walt Whitman and Ralph Waldo Emerson (Taylor 32, 84-87). The sick soul type of religion, he observes, conveys a very different attitude:

> Now in contrast with such healthy-minded views as these, if we treat them as a way of deliberately minimizing evil, stands a radically opposite view, a way of maximizing evil [suffering], if you please so to call it, based on the persuasion that the evil aspects of life are of its very essence, and that the world's meaning most comes home to us when we lay them most to heart. (130-31)

The pervasiveness of evil and absence of meaning engender a sense of melancholy and despair. Consequently, persons with this type of religion have a tendency to take flight from a corrupt world and locate salvation and refuge in a transcendent God.

Taylor summarizes the differences between these two ways of being religious:

> In the first religious schema, the locus of the real "is always in some way *present* here and now. Since it is not elsewhere, the relation to the real is immediate, implicit, or direct and, thus, requires neither intermediaries nor mediation. Though not always obvious, the real is immanent in natural and historial processes as the generative ground and unifying principle. Appearances to the contrary notwithstanding, difference, diversity, and multiplicity are unreal; an original unity is always antecedent to and a condition of the possibility of all separation and division. Differences once articulated can become oppositions, but the unity grounding them is never lost. (37)

This worldview emphasizes immanence; in Christian terms, it is a realized eschatology in which salvation is at hand here and now (39). Some versions of Eastern traditions express monistic worldviews but are beyond the scope of Taylor's analysis of schemas (Buddhist monism or nondualism is discussed below). The religion of the sick soul exemplifies a second way of being religious. According to Taylor:

> The second schema is dualistic: the real is not present here and now but is absent or, more precisely, is elsewhere. In theological terms, the real is transcendent. Such transcendence can be expressed spatially or temporally; accordingly, the real can be conceived, on the one hand, as above or below, on the other hand, as in the past or the future . . . . At the most rudimentary level, the relation—or nonrelation—between the real and the not-real entails the exclusive logic of either/or in which identity is established by opposition to difference. In contrast to the monistic schema, here differences are not finally identical but are constituted oppositionally and, thus, remain irreducible. (39)

The two schemas reflect contrary experiences of being-in-the-world. For monists the real is immanent in nature and history; the self is at home in the world. The challenge facing individuals with this temperament is not to change themselves or the world but to learn to embrace what is as what ought to be (38-39). For dualists, by contrast, there is no direct or essential association with the real; it is not immediate but must be mediated. Since theists conceive of the real as God, relationship to God must be given or revealed through intermediaries like prophets, saints, and messiahs or in rituals and oral and written sacred texts. Taylor summarizes the implications: "Within this schema, the history of religions is, in large measure, the story of competing narratives about various intermediaries, which are constructed to establish and maintain the relation between the real and the not-real" (39). The opposition between the transcendent and the immanent translates into oppositions between good and evil, believers and nonbelievers, the redeemed and the condemned. Taylor notes that this logic of either/or leads to closed systems that make negotiations difficult and compromise nearly often impossible. Moreover, when two religions or ideologies with uncompromising dualistic perspectives encounter one another, the situation becomes dangerous and conducive to violence. Both sides subscribe to a view of history as a struggle with the evil Other; as long as the forces of evil, however they are conceived, go undefeated, things are not as they ought to be (39-40). Individuals and communities find meaning and purpose by participating in the struggle to destroy the darkness of the present age so that a new world order can dawn. Peaceful coexistence in an increasingly globalized world remains an impossible ideal.

Although Taylor finds James's types of religion useful for historical purposes, he finds this twofold typology to be inadequate for understanding the interrelationship of nature, society, and culture. He proposes a third alternative, a schema predicated upon neither/nor logic:

> In contrast to the monistic and dualistic types, the real in this case is neither present nor absent; rather, it is irreducibly interstitial or liminal and as such is *virtual*. It is important to understand the precise meaning of *virtual* in this context. The virtual is not simply the possible but it is the *matrix* in which possibility and actuality emerge. While the logic of monism is both/and and the logic of dualism is either/or, the logic of complexity is neither/nor. Rather than the synthesis or union of the first and the second, the third schema is the condition of their possibility, which they presuppose but cannot include or comprehend . . . . Nothing is either simple or self-identical because everything is codependent and coevolves. Identity and difference, for example, are not oppositional but are thoroughly relational: each is relative to the other, and thus each inhabits and is inhabited by the other. Instead of wrapping identities in a solipsistic shroud, such relativity or, more precisely, *relationalism* draws them out of themselves in a creative play of differences. In this schema, to be is to be related, or in current terms, *to be is to be connected.* (40)

Taylor's alternative schema creates a context in which persons, cultures, and religions can engage each other in a manner that is more conducive to mutual understanding and less prone to intractable conflict. The real is an open-ended and creative process that emerges as ecological, social, cultural, economic, and technological systems evolve in history. The universe embodies *autopoiesis*: it is a self-organizing, infinitely creative, indeterminate process. The end or goal is always emerging by forever withdrawing. This is the context in which the title of his book may be understood. *After* refers not only to the death of the traditional Western God-image; it is also what we are restlessly moving towards through acts of personal and cultural creativity. As Taylor expresses it, "To think after God is to think the after that is forever before us" (41).

Taylor's God-image expresses a contemporary form of negative theology, though he prefers the term *a/theology*. His perspective resembles Buddhism, though it emerges entirely from thinking about the trajectory of Western religious thought. His God-image is a "groundless ground," a phrase that evokes the Buddhist notion of emptiness (*shunyata*), an originary abyss from which everything emerges. He notes that while this abyss is no thing, it is not nothing; rather, it is the condition of the possibility of creative emergence and is the basis for an affirmative vision of life (345). On this basis, Taylor argues for "a religion without God" (that is, without a traditional theistic God-image) and an "ethics without absolutes." Since life is thoroughly interrelated in a global web, nurturing it requires the acceptance of religious and secular worldviews that support our complex interconnections rather than ideologies that reinforce divisive oppositions. Cooperation must complement competition if we are to create the new global institutions necessary to regulate the natural, social, cultural, and technological currents that make life possible. Taylor maintains that, "within these fluxes and flows, nothing is absolute because everything is related" (376). To affirm this possibility, however impossible it may seem in the context of conflicting nations and environmental crises like global warming, requires risking a faith that embraces uncertainty and insecurity as conditions of creative emergence. Such a faith is a vital alternative to that of the neofoundationalists of different religious traditions for whom life in this world is not intrinsically valuable, but has meaning and purpose only insofar as it prepares the way for the eternal life yet to come.

C. G. Jung's concept of the God-image and Individuation

The depth psychology of C. G. Jung presents a different interpretative response to the death of God in the West. Jung wrote extensively on religion and used the word "God" more than six thousand times in his writings (Dyer x). However, he paid little attention to God as transcending the universe and dealt with images of God that arise in the psyche. Jung recognized the common tendency of people to anthropomorphize or attribute a human form or personality to God. Consequently, he often stated that when he uses the word *God* he is always referring to the *God-image* in the psyche. Jung posited the reality of a God-image as a unifying and transcendent symbol capable of drawing together heterogeneous psychic fragments or uniting polarized opposites. Like an image, the symbol is a psychic product different from the object that it attempts to represent and to which it points. The God-image points to a reality that transcends ego consciousness, is extraordinarily numinous, compels attention, attracts energy, and is analogous to an idea that in similar form has forced itself upon humankind in all parts of the world and in all historical epochs. As such, it is an image of totality and "as the highest value and supreme dominant in the psychic hierarchy, the God-image is immediately related to, or identical with, the self" (*CW* 9ii, para.170).

Jung's perspective was often misunderstood because it requires that a person think about the divine in psychological terms. He wrote, "It is the fault of the everlasting contamination of object and imago that people can make no conceptual distinction between 'God' and 'God-image,' and therefore think that when one speaks of the 'God-image' one is speaking of God and offering 'theological' explanations . . . . It is equally clear that *the God-image corresponds to a definite complex of psychological facts*, and is thus a quantity which we can operate with; but what God is in himself remains a question outside the competence of all psychology" (*CW* 8, para. 528; italics added). Viewed therapeutically, the God-image functions as "a church within" or psychic container; it is a frame of reference and system of values by which one lives. He accepted as a God-image whatever an individual claimed to experience as God; it is that which presents a person's highest value, whether expressed consciously or unconsciously (Samuels, Shorter and Prout 61-62).

The Epistemological Basis of Jung's Psychology

The second volume of Jung's letters, from 1951 to 1961, which covers the last ten years of his life, contains a series of letters that reflect upon the nature of the Western God-image and the transformation it is undergoing for modern persons who consciously participate in the individuation process. Edward Edinger, one of the foremost commentators on Jung's major works, assembled a selection of these letters that analyzes the epistemological premises underlying Jung's conception of the evolving God-image. The critical philosophy of Immanuel Kant was central to Jung's psychology; his theory of knowledge is the threshold that must be crossed if the God-image is to be understood in psychological terms. As Jung expressed in a letter to Bernard Lang: "On that threshold minds go their separate ways: those that have understood Kant, and the others who cannot follow him" (*Letters* 375). Human subjectivity and the beginning of modern consciousness began around 1500. In effect, the God-image fell out of heaven into the human psyche and, since then, we have become conscious of the subjectivity of experience and can no longer grant it metaphysical validity (Edinger 3). All experience is subjective or psychological; all is an experience of the soul because nothing can be experienced except through the psyche. For a given individual, this is either self-evident or it is not; it is an issue concerning the perception of the nature of human experience (9). Jung's epistemological stance also entails a non-dogmatic attitude regarding one's own religious convictions and a pluralistic acceptance of views different from one's own. As Jung explained, "My human limitation does not permit me to assert that I know God, hence I cannot but regard all assertions about God as relative because subjectively conditioned—and this out of respect for my brothers, whose other conceptions and beliefs have as much to justify them as mine" (*Letters* 376).

Jung's interest in religion is focused on direct experience rather than doctrines and beliefs. His father was a Protestant minister and it was his experience of his father's crisis of faith that led him to rely on his own experience. Jung wrote: "It was the tragedy of my youth to see my father cracking up before my eyes on the problem of faith and dying an early death" (*Letters* 257; *Memories* 91-96). He further characterized his own approach as similar to the Apostle Paul's experience in the New Testament:

> I was thrown back on experience alone. Always Paul's experience on the road to Damascus hovered before me. Yet this experience came upon him while he was blindly pursuing his own way. As a young man I drew the conclusion that you must obviously fulfill your destiny in order to get to the point where a *donum gratiae* might happen along. But I was far from certain, and always kept the possibility in mind that this road might end up in a black hole. I have remained true to this attitude all my life. From this you can easily see the origin of my own psychology: only by going my own way, integrating my capacities headlong (like Paul), and thus creating a foundation for myself, could something be vouchsafed to me or built upon it. (*Letters* 257)

The courage to find one's own way is the path of individuation, which is, in my view, a form of postmodern spirituality.

Individuation and the Journey to Wholeness

Individuation, for Jung, is the process by which a person differentiates from others and becomes a unique individual. At a deeper level, it may also be described as the path to wholeness and it is the ultimate concern of Jung's psychology; it is the *opus* or work of a lifetime. The process of individuation, when consciously pursued, leads to the realization of the Self as a psychic reality greater than the ego. Jung's own process of individuation is exemplified in experiences he recounts in his memoir, *Memories, Dreams, Reflections*. Jung experienced a midlife crisis after the demise of his close friendship and collegial relationship with Sigmund Freud, just prior to the outbreak of World War I. The period that followed was one of isolation and inner chaos wherein Jung was assailed by material that made him doubt his own sanity. These were the years of his confrontation with the unconscious. Throughout this time, he carefully observed and documented the dreams, fantasies, and visions that are now available to us in *The Red Book*. As he made mandala drawings and understood their significance, he began to emerge from his inner darkness. As an image arising from the unconscious that takes place in times of psychic disorganization, the mandala offers the psyche a way of restoring balance and order. As his psychic state changed, so did the mandalas. As Jung explained:

> I was being compelled to go through this process of the unconscious. I had to let myself be carried along by the current, without a notion of where it would lead me. When I began drawing the mandalas, however, I saw that everything, all the paths I had been following, all the steps I had taken, were leading back to a single point—namely, the midpoint. It became increasingly plain to me that the mandala is the center. It is the exponent of all paths. It is the path to the center, to individuation. (*Memories* 196)

This insight gave Jung stability and gradually restored his inner peace and it held great significance for his life and his psychology. As Jung put it, "I knew that in finding the mandala as an expression of the self I had attained what was for me the ultimate. Perhaps someone else knows more, but not I" (197). Thus, the mandala symbolized for Jung the ultimate goal of the individuation process: the realization of the Self and the attainment of wholeness.

Jung's entire psychology centers upon the relationship between the ego and the unconscious, although this relationship is often a problematic one. The first half of life involves ego development accompanied by progressive separation between the ego and the Self. The second half of life, however, requires the surrender or relativization of the ego as it establishes a reconnection to the Self through dialogical processes such as dream work and active imagination. The conscious work of individuation requires, from a psychological standpoint, a "religious attitude" or careful and scrupulous observation of one's psychological life (Von Franz 201). The process entails an effort to discover the Self and to keep attuned to it so that it becomes an inner partner toward whom one's attention is continually turned (Raff 2-13). In this way, Jung's psychology can function as a religious path, especially for individuals who are no longer able to find meaning in traditional religions. For such persons, neither sin nor redemption, nor ignorance and wisdom, but fragmentation and wholeness form the center of the religious quest (C. Smith 118).

The Evolution of the Western God-Image

Jung believed that the God-image has evolved in the cultural history of the West. Edinger's commentary on Jung's conception of this evolution delineates six stages and serves as an additional context for understanding the significance of Jung's concept of individuation. In the earliest stage of *animism*, the autonomous psyche is experienced in a diffuse way: autonomous spirits are present in animals, trees, places, and rivers. An elemental psychology is immersed in its environment and surroundings. In the next stage of *matriarchy*, the great, nourishing earth-mother is the primary factor: the psychology of this stage is exemplified in vegetation symbolism, fertility rites, and death and rebirth imagery. With the emergence of cities comes the third stage of *hierarchical polytheism*, in which the masculine principle begins to supercede the feminine principle. A family of deities emerges with a patriarchal sky-god at the head. The polytheism of Mesopotamia, Egypt, and Greece exemplifies this, as do the mythologies of Norse and Germanic peoples. Written scriptures also emerge in this stage. The fourth stage is *tribal monotheism*: out of the many deities of the ancient Near East, Yahweh emerges as the single, all-encompassing One for the ancient Hebrews. Although He is the creator of the universe and governor of all, He has personal relations only with the chosen people. He has enemies both among and outside his chosen people. There is a latent dualism in the God-image even though monotheism is insisted upon. With the emergence of Christianity, *universal monotheism*, the fifth stage, occurs when the tribal monotheism of ancient Israel is universalized and becomes available to all nations. However, for Jung, this new God-image was split into two in the course of it becoming an all-good image: Israel's Yahweh is a Father-God and Christianity's God-image is a Son-God. Also, in Jung's account of this stage, Yahweh has two sons: Christ and Satan. In order for Yahweh to turn into the all-good Christ, he had to split off the all-bad Satan who remains lurking around to be dealt with sooner or later (a problem dealt with by Jung in his *Answer to Job*). Finally, *individuation* is the sixth and last stage in this long process of cultural evolution: here religious imagery is understood to be an expression of the phenomenology of the objective psyche. To perceive this new God-image, a person must master the Kantian-Jungian epistemological premises discussed above, which enable a person to recognize the reality of the psyche. Then, as the God-image lives itself out in one's own psychology, as well as in the psychology of the collective, one becomes aware of all one can to help in the process of the further transformation of this God-image. For Jung, this is the process of continuing incarnation. In other words, the God-image has become fully immanent in the psyche and human beings become the instrument of its further development in personal and cultural life (xv-xxii).

Although the stages in the evolution of the God-image described above depict a linear process in the history of the West, psychological growth has the quality of a spiral in which one circles or revisits fragments of psychological material until they can be integrated. Jung described this process as *circumambulation*:

> The goal of this approximation seems to be anticipated by archetypal symbols which represent something like the circumambulation of the centre. With increasing approximation to the centre there is a corresponding depotentiation of the ego in favour of the influence of the "empty" center, which is certainly not identical with the archetype but is the thing to which the archetype points to. As the Chinese would say, the archetype is only a name of Tao, not the Tao itself. Just as the Jesuits translated Tao as "God," so we can describe this "emptiness" of the centre as "God." Emptiness in this sense doesn't mean "absence" or "vacancy," but something which is endowed with the highest intensity. (*Letters* 258).

This passage has implications for understanding the God-images of different religious traditions. Jung envisioned the ultimate as "empty" in the sense that it is beyond any particular cultural or religious system of symbols. Such a view supports genuine religious pluralism: the affirmation that different religions and their symbols and names for the ultimate are valid, yet none are absolute. Although emptiness is a term used by Buddhists to describe ultimate reality, it is also applicable in a Western context. Here "the emptiness of the centre" has a psychological significance: it counters exclusivist and fundamentalist attitudes that engender opposition and conflict between persons with different religious beliefs. Individuation leads to inclusivity and the vision of the *unus mundus*, the unitary world shared by all of humanity that encompasses diversity.

The Divine Feminine

Jung recognized that the feminine had been repressed in the Christian God-image. He regarded the Catholic dogma regarding the Assumption of Mary, defined by Pope Pius XII in 1950, to be a significant development within Catholic Christianity that reflects an incipient effort towards reintegrating the feminine into its conception of divinity (*CW* 11, para. 748). Jungian analyst Marion Woodman has made the theme of the return of the divine feminine a central feature of her work. In *Leaving My Father's House: A Journey to Conscious Femininity*, she writes:

> The eternal feminine is thrusting her way into contemporary consciousness. Shekinah, Kwan Yin, Sophia, whatever her name, she is the manifestation of the divine in matter. Among her many faces are Black Madonna, White Buffalo Woman, Shakti, Kali, Aphrodite. Hers are the ways of peace, compassion, reverence for life and death in oneness of nature. Knowing her has nothing to do with blindly stumbling toward a fate we think we cannot avoid. It has everything to do with developing consciousness until it is strong enough to hold tension as creative energy. In the turmoil of our time, we are being called to a new order of reality . . . . It is our immediate

task to relate to the emerging feminine whether she comes to
us in dreams, in the loss of those we love, in body disease, or in
ecological distress. (1)

Woodman observes that the divine feminine is present in a wide
variety of images found in Christian, Jewish, Chinese, Greek, Hindu,
and Native American traditions. As we recover the plethora of goddess
images, it may be better to speak of the God/dess image as a means of
acknowledging that the divine has long been imaged as both masculine
and feminine. Woodman's comment also helps us overcome a cultural
and historical bias, prevalent not only in the West, that the divine is
located only in spirit.

For Woodman, conscious femininity is not bound to gender. Her
work focuses on the masculine and the feminine as different energies
present in all human beings that need to be integrated in order for
the individuation process to achieve its ultimate goal of wholeness.
However, this integration is difficult to achieve in the context of a
patriarchal culture in which the feminine has been eclipsed. Woodman
conceives of patriarchy in terms of a power principle, an energy that
has damaged both masculine and feminine values. Woodman's God-
image does not replace a male or masculine image with a female or
feminine image; rather, she evokes *sacred marriage* imagery: Yin/Yang,
Shakti/Shiva, Doing/Being (1-2). She is concerned with an image of
the divine that locates divinity in matter, the body, and in dreams. She
seeks to shift the locus of the divine from transcendence and spirit to
immanence and nature. Conscious femininity, in her view, has to do
with bringing the wisdom in nature to consciousness (1-2).

In a documentary of her life and work, Woodman describes the
destructive aspects of her inherited Christian God-image and how
that image has evolved through her Jungian work. She suffered from
an "addiction to perfection" that was the source of a life-threatening
eating disorder. At the root of the addiction was the God-image she
had internalized from Christianity. Andrew Harvey, the interviewer,
asked her, "Who was your killer?" Woodman answered, "It was God,"
meaning "a desire for a kind of perfection that rejects life" (*Marion
Woodman*). Recovery from addiction required devotion to a new

God-image. Woodman encountered the divine feminine during a trip to India when she became gravely ill. She experienced the Black Madonna through the healing presence of a woman who sat near her, body to body, flesh touching flesh, as she recovered. In the interview, she describes the critical element in the healing she had experienced: "Something had to be destroyed in order for me to give up my ego plans. I had to give up the perfection and what I would call the golden spirit that wanted whatever I thought perfection was. I had to completely let go."

The Black Madonna is an archetypal image of the divine that is present not only in certain Christian depictions of Mary but also in the powerful figure of Kali from Hindu tradition. She is, for Woodman, the sacredness in matter that manifests in sexuality, childbirth, and nature—the earthiest aspects of womanhood; she is also the mother of the divine son who embodies a new consciousness in the darkness that holds the light (*Coming Home* 122-23). While this image is central to Woodman's inflection of Jung's psychology, she also embraces Sophia as another aspect of the divine feminine. Within some Christian traditions, Sophia is the aspect of spirituality thought of as feminine wisdom. Woodman teaches that Sophia's wisdom is rooted in experience and expressed in compassion. She is concerned with processes; she does not value the presence of power but the power of presence. Ultimately, Woodman's path to wholeness aims at achieving the inner or sacred marriage, a union that integrates the authentic forms of the masculine and feminine. As she explains, "The true masculine is not the enemy of the feminine; it is not into power . . . . The masculine is the sword of discrimination needed to protect the feminine (including the feminine in man). The strong masculine is needed to love and protect the embodied feminine." In her view, "reconciling these opposites is the key to a new birth, which all great religions are working towards" (*Marion Woodman*). Woodman's God/dess image provides a powerful model of postmodern spirituality informed by Jungian depth psychology, an image that evolves in ways that are particular to each person's individuation process.

Religious Pluralism and Postmodern Spirituality

Religious Pluralism

Pluralism has several meanings depending on the context of its usage. The first pertains to the descriptive fact that there exist within society many groups that are distinct from one another in significant ways. There are within America, for example, many religious communities. A second meaning focuses on doctrinal differences: in this instance, pluralism denotes a diversity of perspectives in contrast to a single viewpoint or method of interpreting reality. The doctrines of different religions express alternative visions. Yet another meaning is philosophical or theological: a theoretical perspective that accepts the validity of differing worldviews and that proposes how they can coexist without threatening one another. While all three meanings are entailed in the discussion that follows, my primary concern is with the latter meaning and its implications for postmodern spirituality.

While awareness of religious pluralism challenges the plausibility of our inherited traditions, it also increases our options. In matters of religion, people are faced not only with the opportunity but also with the necessity of choosing what to believe and how to live meaningful lives. In effect, contemporary life forces individuals to consider many religious alternatives as they search for a belief system or to reject religion altogether and adopt a secular philosophy of life. In more traditional times, when there was greater religious certainty, such deliberate reflection about the meaning of religious belief systems was unnecessary. Sociologist Peter Berger describes this existential responsibility as the heretical imperative, since the word heresy, from the Greek verb *hairein*, means "to choose" (25).

Berger identifies three responses by theologians to the multiple options for belief in contemporary culture. One response reasserts the authority of religious tradition, in the face of modern secularity, to deflect challenges to traditional beliefs. This approach attempts to separate the concerns of religion from science and other forms of secular discourse. When successful, this kind of religious thought minimizes doubt and uncertainty for the faithful; however, it can be rigid, defensive, and conducive to fundamentalism. An alternative response is to reinterpret religious beliefs in secular terms. Rather than resist modernity, it makes traditional religious beliefs intelligible in the contemporary world. Rudolf Bultmann's method of demythologizing Christian beliefs is perhaps the best example of this approach. He replaces mythical interpretations of reality, such as the traditional vision of heaven, earth, and hell, with ideas appropriated from modern existentialism. God is reconceived as the Ground of Being and faith is understood in terms of authenticity. This strategy has the advantage of reducing cognitive dissonance in the self-conscious believer, although the religious content of the tradition often tends to dissolve in the process of translation. A third response is to ground religious affirmations in experience. Focusing on the experiences that underlie religious doctrines, this style of religious thought is non-dogmatic and empirical in character. C. G. Jung and William James, among others, advocated this third approach.

Postmodern Spirituality

Postmodern is another term with multiple meanings depending on the context. With respect to historical epochs, postmodern refers to the contemporary context of globalization characterized by the interrelatedness of economic, technological, and communication systems. In addition, I use the term to describe the implications of pluralism: the recognition that no single narrative or theory, either religious or secular, can adequately understand the complexity of human lives and cultures. I am not, however, referring to the movement of thought within academic disciplines such as literary studies and philosophy known as deconstruction. The deconstructive mode of interpretation emphasizes the social construction of reality and philosophical relativism. One aim of deconstruction is to decode the meanings inherent in a text—broadly conceived to include all social and cultural phenomena—and their instability; another is to reveal how knowledge systems are used to legitimate the interests of dominant groups in society. This volume of essays, by contrast, regards the God-images of people as expressions of their ultimate concerns and values. To be postmodern, in this sense, is to engage in a constructive style of thought that affirms the existence of transcultural values; it can be described more aptly as non-absolutism rather than relativism. Religious or spiritual truths, instead of being merely personal or exclusive to a particular tradition or community, can convey wisdom that belongs to our shared humanity. As the historian of religions, Wilfred Cantwell Smith put it his book *Towards a World Theology*, "Our solidarity precedes our particularity, and is part of our self-transcendence. The truth of all of us is part of the truth of each of us" (79).

Spirituality is a term that traditionally refers to the contemplative form of a religion practiced primarily by monastics. In recent decades, the meaning of the term has expanded to include forms of religiosity that are grounded in direct experience rather than doctrinal belief. For instance, as the preceding section discussed, Jung's concept of individuation as a path to wholeness functions, for many persons, as a depth psychological form of spirituality. This is true for those who remain affiliated with a religious tradition, finding deeper meanings in it through the Jungian interpretation of its myths and symbols, as well as for individuals who engage depth psychology without directly participating in a tradition.

The latter approach is part of a larger and growing trend in which people regard themselves to be "spiritual but not religious." There are also advocates of atheistic spirituality who maintain that spirituality can be grounded in values that are understood entirely in secular terms. Both religious and non-religious persons have long embraced values like *truth, goodness, beauty, justice, love,* and *compassion.* Religious pluralism has been present since ancient times and, in the East, includes atheistic or non-theistic religions such as Buddhism and Jainism. Thus, the Western assumption that religion and atheism are antithetical is a cultural bias that loses its meaning as soon as one becomes aware of the teachings and practices of the world's diverse religious traditions. What is new about religious pluralism is not only the simple fact of many religions and worldviews; it is our heightened awareness of the novel situation in which these different visions of life coexist in a given culture. American society, for instance, is no longer comprised primarily of Jews, Catholics, and Protestants, but hosts virtually every large-scale religion found on the planet, as well as smaller indigenous traditions. The same holds true in European countries and in pluralistic nations like India in the East.

Postmodern spirituality is distinguished by reliance upon direct experience and practice rather than belief. Here, practice refers to contemplative and psychological activities that an individual engages to cultivate integration and wholeness in one's personality and for enacting values such as love and compassion towards sentient beings. The discussion of religion and secularity shifts from the predominately Western frames of analysis, exemplified by Mark C. Taylor and C. G. Jung, to the Buddhist perspective on religious pluralism and secularity offered by His Holiness the Dalai Lama. I regard his earnest efforts to foster inter-religious harmony and an ethics for a global society to be an exemplary contribution towards achieving these important aims.

The Dalai Lama's Personal Journey

In 1959, at the age of twenty-four, the Dalai Lama was forced to escape from Tibet to India. The political circumstances that drove him into exile still prevent him from returning to his native land (ix). His life is an extraordinary example of how a person may come to embrace religious pluralism. When he came to India as a refugee, he knew very little about religions other than his native Buddhism. During the past fifty years, he has devoted much of his time and attention to learning about the world's religions (xiv). He acknowledges that when he was growing up, he thought Buddhism was the best religion; no other faith tradition, he felt, could rival its depth, sophistication, and inspirational power. All other religions, by comparison, must be "so-so." Looking back, he is embarrassed by his naiveté, which could only be sustained as long as he was isolated from any real contact with other religions (1-2). During his first visit to India, where he encountered Jains, Hindus, and members of the Theosophical Society in Madras, he described himself as "a changed man." He could no longer live in the comfort of an exclusivist standpoint that takes Buddhism to be the only true religion. As he explains, his exposure to the grandeur of India's great religions enabled him "to let go of the mental comfort zone, a space where my own Buddhism was the one true religion and other faith traditions were at best mere similitude" (6-7). His life is a testament to how we too may move from the comfort zone of our inherited faith traditions in order to understand the millions of our fellow human beings who live in accordance with worldviews that may seem so different from our own.

Among the first Christians the Dalai Lama encountered, as he committed himself to understanding other faith traditions, was Thomas Merton, a Catholic Trappist monk. Merton, who visited the Dalai Lama in Dharmasala just three months before his own tragic accidental death, opened his eyes to the richness and depth of the Christian faith and to an appreciation of Christianity that has continued to deepen in his engagement with other Christians committed to inter-religious dialogue. Merton, he felt, showed great courage in exploring traditions beyond his own; his attitude for exploring them was exemplary, penetrating so deeply that he could "taste the actual flavor of the teachings that other traditions represent" (9).

The Challenge of Peaceful Existence

Why does the Dalai Lama give such great importance to the cultivation of inter-religious understanding? His answer is that the future of humanity—even of the planet—depends upon it. We live in a world that is truly global and interdependent. "The challenge of peaceful co-existence," he believes, "will define the task of humanity in the twenty-first century" (x). The line between exclusivism, which regards one's own religion to be the only legitimate one, and fundamentalism is a dangerously narrow one; the line between fundamentalism and extremism is even narrower. After 9/11, he observes, the upholding of exclusivist religious bigotry in the world is no longer a private matter of an individual's personal outlook; it has the potential to affect the lives of all. The lesson he draws is clear: understanding and harmony between the world's religions is one of the essential preconditions for genuine world peace (xi-xii).

Accepting the legitimacy of other faith traditions poses a threat to many religious persons because it challenges their commitment to their own faith (145). How can a single-pointed commitment to one's faith be reconciled with the acceptance of other religions as equally legitimate? Many people feel that the answer to this question requires the acceptance of some kind of ultimate unity of religions. Adherents of Vedanta, for example, often affirm this unity using the metaphor of multiple rivers converging into the great ocean. Others suggest that the world's religions, though exhibiting distinct beliefs and practices, all ultimately lead to the same place. That place may be union with the Godhead, regardless of how differently this Godhead is named or described (Yahweh, God, Ishvara, Allah, or by other names) (147). The problem with these approaches, the Dalai Lama argues, is that all religions are not, in fact, the same. Consequently, recognizing the diversity among the world's faiths is not only essential, but is also the first step toward creating deeper understanding of each. As he explains, "True understanding of the 'other' must proceed from a genuine recognition and respect for the other's reality" (147). Such understanding requires a state of mind that resists the strong tendency to reduce and fit the other into one's own framework. Like it or not, he asserts, the existence of other religions is an undeniable fact. Furthermore, the teachings of the great religions provide great benefits to their adherents (148). His position is realistic in acknowledging that it is simply impossible for the six billion human inhabitants on our planet to embrace a single religious tradition (148).

The reasoning that supports the Dalai Lama's pluralistic stance incorporates two other important observations, the first being psychological. Diverse mental dispositions, spiritual inclinations, and conditioning have always been a feature of human society; therefore, no set of spiritual teachings could serve everyone. The second observation is historical. During the long history of the world's religions—in some cases, extending over thousands of years—the religions have evolved into a complex human geography adapted to specific cultural sensibilities and environments that have engendered different habits of mind. These cultural traditions cannot be changed overnight, nor is it desirable that they change. Creating a single world religion, whether a new one or one formed from the old ones, is not feasible (148-49).

In today's globalized world, where the world's religions are now in daily contact, a positive response to pluralism is imperative. The world's religions have often been a source of conflict throughout history, from the Crusades in medieval times to jihad today, as well as the recent phenomenon of religion-inspired terrorism. While acknowledging this historical legacy of violence, the Dalai Lama believes it is time to say that "history is history and that we must now move on." The critical question is not, he says, "Are religions only a source of trouble," but instead, "What can we do to ensure that the differences between religions no longer give birth to divisions and conflicts in society?" (131). As a deep believer in the positive nature of human potential, he is committed to the view that harmony among religions is achievable, but only by promoting genuine understanding between them (132).

The Call for a Secular Ethics Beyond Religion

Although the Dalai Lama is an advocate of religion, he insists that we need a secular ethics in the postmodern world of the twenty-first century. He clearly and forcefully states his conviction on this matter:

> Certainly religion has helped millions of people in the past, helps millions today, and will continue to help millions in the future. But for all of its benefits in offering moral guidance and meaning in life, in today's world religion alone is no longer adequate as a basis for ethics. One reason for this is that many people in the world no longer follow any particular religion. Another reason is that, as the peoples of the world become ever more closely interconnected in an age of globalization and in multicultural societies, ethics based on any one religion would only appeal to some of us; it would not be meaningful for all . . . . Today . . . any religion-based answer to our neglect of inner values can never be universal, and so will be inadequate. What we need today is an approach to ethics which makes no recourse to religion and can be equally acceptable to those

with faith and those without: a secular ethics. (*Beyond Religion* xiii-xiv)

He acknowledges that a call for a secular ethics from a Buddhist religious leader may seem contradictory. However, he explains that his faith enjoins him to strive for the welfare and benefit of all sentient beings; to reach out beyond his own tradition to those with other religions and those with none is entirely in keeping with this obligation. Moreover, he believes "that we have within our grasp a way, and a means, to ground inner values without contradicting any religion and yet, crucially, without depending on religion" (xiv).

Compassion as a Unifying Principle

Given the differences that distinguish religions and those that differentiate religions from secular worldviews, where can we find common ground? The Dalai Lama's deeply held view, the one that pervades his writings, is that compassion is the core of human nature:

> It is my fundamental conviction that compassion—the natural capacity of the human heart to feel concern and connection to another being—constitutes the basic aspect of our nature shared by all human beings .... All ethical teachings, whether religious or nonreligious, aim to nurture this innate and precious quality, to develop it and to perfect it. (*Kinship of Faiths* 109)

He notes that a careful study of religion identifies the Golden Rule as a common ethical principle. Underlying the world religions' moral teachings, it serves as an ethics of constraint: one's behavior should be guided by how one wishes others to behave towards oneself (112). There is also, however, a higher level of ethics contained in the teachings of religions. While the Golden Rule principle serves as the bedrock for civility, a more expansive principle is needed, one that is also contained within teachings of differing religious traditions. "What we find," he observes," is a vision of ethics that moves beyond the limited reciprocity of the Golden Rule to an exhortation to universal compassion . . . . On this level, beyond grounding one's ethics in a *self-referential* framework—that is, "*I* do not do to others what I wish them not to do to *me*'—the world's religions situate this ethics within a larger frame that extends beyond the boundaries of self-reference" (114).

The Compassion Charter

Karen Armstrong received a TED (Technology, Entertainment, Design) award to facilitate the formulation of the Charter for Compassion, a project based on her studies in the history of religions, which closely aligns with the Dalai Lama's teachings. Focusing on the Abrahamic traditions that have had a long history of conflict, her inquiry discerns common ground that can serve as a basis for cooperation rather than strife. Armstrong stresses that belief is a recent religious enthusiasm that emerged in the 17th century. *Belief* meant "to love" and "to hold dear." In this sense, belief is *credo*, a statement of principles that serves as a basis for how to conduct one's life; it means, "I commit myself" or "I engage myself." Religion is about behaving differently. Religious doctrines are summons to action; you only understand them when you put them into practice (*My Wish*).

Expressing views that closely accord with the Dalai Lama's, Armstrong asserts that compassion is the true test of religiosity and that each of the world religions has put the Golden Rule at the core of their ethical teachings. Religions insist that you cannot confine compassion to your own group; we are enjoined, instead, to love our enemies and to welcome the stranger. Any ideology that does not foster global understanding is failing the needs of our time. Although she was once deeply disillusioned by religion, she now believes that it can and should be a force for harmony in the world. On the basis of that conviction she used her award money to work with religious leaders from many traditions to establish the Charter for Compassion. Thousands of people from around the world contributed a draft charter on a multilingual website, in Hebrew, Arabic, Urdu, Spanish, and English. Their comments were presented to a Council of Conscience, a group of notable individuals from six faith traditions (Judaism, Christianity,

Islam, Hinduism, Buddhism, and Confucianism), who met in Switzerland in February, 2009, to compose the final version:

> The principle of compassion lies at the heart of all religious, ethical and spiritual traditions, calling us to always treat others as we wish to be treated ourselves.
>
> Compassion impels us to work tirelessly to alleviate the suffering of our fellow creatures, to dethrone ourselves from the center of our world and put another there, and to honor the inviolable sanctity of every single human being, treating everyone, without exception, with absolute justice, equity and respect.
>
> It is also necessary in both public and private life to refrain consistently and empathetically from inflicting pain. To act or speak violently out of spite, chauvinism or self-interest, to impoverish, exploit or deny basic rights to anybody, and to incite hatred by denigrating others—even our enemies—is a denial of our common humanity. We acknowledge that we have failed to live compassionately and that some have even increased the sum of human misery in the name of religion.
>
> We therefore call upon all men and women
>
> ❖ to restore compassion to the center of morality and religion;
> ❖ to return to the ancient principle that any interpretation of scripture that breeds violence, hatred or disdain is illegitimate;
> ❖ to ensure that youth are given accurate and respectful information about other traditions, religions and cultures;
> ❖ to encourage a positive appreciation of cultural and religious diversity;
> ❖ to cultivate an informed empathy with the suffering of all human beings—even those regarded as enemies. (Armstrong 6-8)

The charter, unveiled on November 12, 2009, in sixty different locations throughout the world, is enshrined in synagogues, mosques, temples, and churches, as well as in secular institutions such as the Karachi Press Club and the Sydney Opera House.

Recent theories of human development also align with the Dalai Lama's teachings and The Compassion Charter. Carol Gilligan, for instance, posits three stages of moral development: selfish, care, and universal care (105, 174). Likewise, Ken Wilber delineates four stages of human development with regard to the scope of concern: egocentric (self), ethnocentric (family, ethnic group, nation), worldcentric (all of humanity), and cosmocentric (the cosmos and all sentient beings). According to such theories, human development, when it unfolds towards maturity, is a trajectory in which people expand their capacity to express care, compassion, and concern (11-13).

I share the conviction that a kinship of religions is possible and that we urgently need to make compassion a "clear, luminous and dynamic force in our polarized world" (Armstrong, TED lecture). Boundaries from the past need to be revisioned. Eastern/Western, religious/secular, masculine/feminine, spiritual/psychological, traditional/individual: these binary aspects of life are not opposites but complementary aspects of culture and the psyche. No person, culture or nation is an island unto itself: to be is to be related. We are enjoined to make the journey from our ecocentric and ethnocentric comfort zones to compassionate concern for others in our profoundly interconnected world. To answer this call, we must strive to understand the worldviews of others who differ from us but who nonetheless yearn to live in a more peaceful, just, and sustainable world. The willingness to embrace this challenge is the work of conscious individuation and is the heart of any life-affirming spirituality. The death of God is not a nihilistic dead end; it heralds the birth of postmodern God-images that affirm our shared humanity, the divine feminine, and the divinity that inheres in nature.

The Essays

Theistic and Monistic Spirituality

Many of the essayists is this section had Christian upbringings of some kind and retain aspects of their heritage, though their God-images have changed as they have moved through life. Some of the essays affirm God-images that are personal and theistic; others affirm more monistic and panentheistic conceptions of the divine. (Panentheism differs from pantheism by affirming that divinity both transcends nature and pervades it.) All of the contributors ground their spirituality in experience and convey a pluralistic attitude of acceptance with regard to how others understand the divine.

In a personal story that begins with a powerful memory of God's presence at the age of three, Julia Stone Berg traces the evolution of her ever-expanding God-image. She tells us that she did not find God, but that God found her. This loving and protective presence enabled her to survive the challenging reality of her home life as a child and a traumatic accident and near-death experience in her early twenties; it continues to enliven her soul in her seventies. Her journey with institutional religion, which began within Catholicism, included compassionate mentoring from a nun and a priest. When Catholicism was no longer viable for her, she became an Episcopalian after exploring many Christian churches. In her fifties, she left the confines of organized religion, moving more deeply into spirituality without boundaries. As she puts it, "I am now free to belong anywhere and everywhere." Even so, she tells us that she continues to chisel away at remnants of a God-image that no longer serves her. Now in her seventies, that image continues to grow as she accepts life more completely and trusts in the unfathomable but constant presence that animates. Berg also offers reflections on how her introverted temperament influences her spirituality.

Reflection upon the evolution of the Western God-image is the focus of Susan Chaney's theoretical essay. She effectively conjoins the depth psychological insights of C. G. Jung and Edward Edinger with Mark C. Taylor's analysis of the dynamics of religion in the context of the postmodern world. The common theme among these theorists is the need to create order and meaning out of chaos. She shows how chaos is an integral aspect of creative emergence, an opportunity to birth new forms and expand worldviews. In a context of unprecedented technological change, she observes that images of God are becoming less rigid and more dynamic. At the same time, popular images of contemporary culture depict consumerism, sexuality, and power—images that are superficial and cut us off from inner depth, triggering the contrary reactions of fundamentalism and secularization. Her essay makes an eloquent plea for investigating dualistic responses to complexity and chaos. In her view, Jung's emphasis on individuation complements the Dalai Lama's focus on compassion and respect for others. These values are key to creating a future that fosters mutual respect and understanding rather then divisiveness and strife.

The role of imagination and image is the focus of D. Maggie Dowdy's understanding of the divine. Raised as a Catholic, she discovered that Catholicism is just one of the many forms of Christianity and that Christianity is but one of many religions. By midlife, she doubted whether any religion could make claims to absolute knowledge. Like Jung, she came to embrace the Kantian idea that it is impossible to "know God;" we can only image and define God within the limitations of our human imagination. From a Jungian perspective, however, this limitation does not preclude one from experiencing the numinous. Rather, it has engendered a pluralistic understanding of religion that embraces differences even when doctrinal beliefs clash. In her own case, she experiences God as divine energy, which she eloquently describes as "remote in its mystery out there, yet permeating and informing our very presence in the here and now."

In a deeply personal story, Daniel Gurska reveals how religion can heal childhood wounds and traumas. As a teenager, he experienced the power of love at a Methodist summer camp, an experience that assuaged his existential aloneness. As an adult, his spiritual quest has been nourished by the study of myth and religion. Through these studies, he has discovered that teachings of love and compassion are the common threads that surround the God archetype; this he describes as the Eros drive. His self-reflection also takes account of his psychological type or temperament and how it shapes his God-image, which he describes as the discovery of the divine through connection with others. While his image of the divine may no longer be distinctly Christian, the New Testament notion that God is love persists in his affirmation of the divine as a form of relational love.

Lynlee Lyckberg imagines that the divine, a mystery unknowable by rational means, is immanent in everything. She ponders the implications, asking, "What if God is one of us?" or "What if God is all of us?" Although she is not a traditional theist, her essay reveals a religious attitude. Like Jung and Edinger, she acknowledges that our conceptions of God are anthropomorphic and mythic, but cannot relinquish her need to be cared for by "the imaginary beloved who goes by the name God." She meets this need through painting. Making art, for her, is a form of visual prayer; it is her way to commune with the divine. She describes her God-image as an energy field and as pure being. Her way of relating to this transpersonal presence aligns with her typology. As an intuitive type, she apprehends the world through intuition, with thinking as a supporting function, a mode of perception that enables her to hear God in the wind rustling through the trees and to see God in the faces of everyone around her.

Emmanuelle Patrice adheres to a panentheistic conception of the divine. As a child, her Baptist upbringing exposed her to members of her congregation who had ecstatic experiences of the Holy Spirit. When her mother remarried into a Catholic family, she witnessed a form of Christianity that mediates the Spirit through sacraments. As an adult, after concluding that organized religion primarily serves social, economic, and political interests, she decided that Martin Luther was correct in his assertion that faith is a personal relationship between an individual self and God. She is a strong advocate of the spirituality of the individual and quite pluralistic with regard to what form that may take. She has come to believe that God is not a being but an energy that is efficacious in all processes that animate the cosmos and the psyche. Her God-image is impersonal and theosophical: the Spirit behind all substances, the One from which all diversity emanates. This monistic vision, she feels, is best expressed in the gnostic words of Jesus in the

Gospel of Thomas, words that affirm the presence of Divine Spirit in all forms.

Postmodern faith and ethics are the focus of April Rasmussen's reflections on the problem of absolutes and relativism in contemporary culture. Raised in a progressive Lutheran church, her spiritual identity was also shaped by her father's love-based, non-dogmatic spirituality. She has fashioned a faith without absolutes that does not succumb to nihilistic relativism. To the contrary, she concurs with Mark C. Taylor's conviction that relativism need not be a subjectivism and that it entails a relationalism that supports a deep understanding of the interdependent nature of our world. Rasmussen looks to Martin Luther for a model that supports the ethics needed in the postmodern world. While we are free to relate to the divine as we wish in our private life, our public life requires an ethics that supports the well-being of the collective community. The relational aspect of faith is, for her, the creative aspect of spirituality, the unifying force of love or, in religious language, God.

Elizabeth Wolterink's essay is an inspiring affirmation of both Christian theism and religious pluralism. Her own heritage includes family members from Calvinist Dutch Reform, Presbyterian, and Greek Orthodox traditions. She herself was baptized in the United Church of Christ, confirmed in the Lutheran church, and currently teaches in the Episcopal Church. As a self-described liberal and pluralist Christian, she discloses that she has been deeply nourished by Goddess spirituality, Native American religion, Zen Buddhism, and Hinduism. This mixture of influences, however, is far from being an ungrounded and eclectic spirituality. On the contrary, Wolterink articulates a robust Trinitarian theology that affirms how God encompasses three modes of being. As she explains, God is *transcendent* (neither male or female and beyond form); God is *immanent* in the universe through all matter and the energies that animate its processes (expressing the feminine aspect of divinity); and God is *incarnate* in Jesus (a masculine expression of the deity). She contrasts her theology with Mark C. Taylor's analysis of transcendence and immanence (a neither/nor model), finding her own panentheistic vision to be more akin to the process philosophy of Alfred North

Whitehead. As a religious educator, she shows her students how to understand these complex ideas experientially while, simultaneously, opening her students' eyes to other spiritual paths.

The Divine Feminine and Goddess Spirituality

Several essayists give great importance to the divine feminine and goddess spirituality, each in their own way. Feminism, the immanence of the divine, and ecological concerns are common themes in the essays contained in this section. Several of the essays express a yearning to conjoin feminine and masculine aspects of divinity into a sacred marriage that engenders wholeness in the psyche.

The divine has been a constant, mysterious presence in Alexandra Dragin's life since childhood. Initially, her God-image was grounded in the Christian tradition of Eastern Orthodoxy. God was a good, powerful, loving and benevolent father, and creator of all that exists. As she matured, she was troubled by the patriarchal attitudes of her church and began searching for new images and paths through studies in art, literature, and myth. Fascinating new worlds opened up for her, especially images of the divine feminine: Aphrodite, Athena, and Demeter. Encountering these goddesses through a mythic and psychological perspective was profoundly liberating for her, though she has not abandoned her religion or former masculine God-image. As a pluralist, all of these images co-exist in her psyche. As her spirituality continues to evolve, Dragin embraces the notion of a sacred marriage of spirit (masculine, light, air) and soul (feminine, dark, earth), a God-image that unites the transcendent and immanent aspects of the divine.

Goddess spirituality is an important ingredient in what Clara Oropeza describes as a multifarious practice of prayer to a divinity that has many faces. The foundation of her spirituality is steeped in the Catholicism of the Mexican culture of her childhood. The display of religious icons of the crucified Jesus and saints in her relatives' homes created an atmosphere of mystery. Most of all, she was deeply moved by her grandmother's devotion to the Virgin de Guadalupe, a powerful national symbol of liberation, motherly protection, and love. The God-image of her Catholic upbringing faded during her early adulthood and was replaced with a deep longing to be in the presence of the divine—with all that is divine. While she now integrates practices from indigenous traditions, qigong, yoga, and Buddhist vipassana meditation, her essay emphasizes the centrality of feminism and goddess mythology in her spirituality and her writing. Above all, Oropeza yearns to express the marriage of the divine feminine and masculine in her works as a teacher, a writer, and a woman on a quest towards wholeness.

Identifying herself as a pagan and a witch, April Heaslip describes the formative events in her life that shaped her Gaian cosmology. Through her participation in a Women's Circle and graduate study in ecofeminism and sustainability, she formulated values that grounded her earth-based spirituality, integrating her belief in the existence of gods, goddesses, and ancestors with the conviction that all land is sacred. Participation in a Witch Camp added depth and breadth to her worldview, notably, a commitment to uniting spirituality and activism. Her ecofeminist and Goddess-centered pagan community embraces diversity in relation to ritual worship, religious traditions, and gender identity. Rituals embody mythic themes such as the s/hero's journey and depth psychological work involving shadow material, dreams, and active imagination. Heaslip observes that Witch Camp was a crash course in *applied* Jungian and archetypal cosmology, an immersion experience that has been deepened by her doctoral studies in mythology and depth psychology at Pacifica Graduate Institute. Through the latter, she has discovered that Jung's notion of archetypes is fully congruent with her earth-based spirituality in which she apprehends the sacred as immanent.

As a child, Laurie Larsen experienced the immanence of the sacred in nature. During her adolescence, she noticed the feminine aspect of the divine was missing in the Presbyterian Church in which she was raised. The subservient role of women was troubling and Christianity was no longer viable for her. She entered a long period of feeling bereft of any meaningful connection to the divine until she became a mother. The birth of her children provided a powerful rediscovery of the sacred feminine through the vessel of her own body. Suddenly she felt a direct, vibrant presence of the divine feminine all around her. Her spirituality has become profoundly relational: a vision of life that is interdependent and that recovers the immanence of the divine she experienced in childhood. Like other essayists in this section, Larsen believes that we need a postmodern spirituality that joins the sacred feminine and sacred masculine if we are to survive the ecological problems engendered by the devaluation of nature.

Eastern and Contemplative Spirituality

Immanence is also a central theme in the essays in this section, though the emphasis here is upon accessing the divine by going within, through meditation, contemplation, and prayer. The God-images expressed by essayists include Brahman, the all-pervasive reality affirmed by Hindus; the Buddhist notion of emptiness (*shunyata*), the groundless ground of form; and the Tao, the Chinese image of the harmony of the opposites. Essayists also find divinity not only within their interiority, but also in the beauty of nature and the love expressed in intimate relationships.

In an essay that affirms the immanence of the divine, Jacqueline Fry describes how her God-image has shifted during her life from dependence on a transcendent Other to a divinity dwelling within her heart. She credits Jung's depth psychology in helping her go beyond the tendency to anthropomorphize her conception of divinity. Likewise, she explains that Joseph Campbell's approach to mythology provides an alternative way to understand religious stories. When mythic stories and images are seen symbolically, they point beyond themselves and enable a person to connect to one's bliss and to find where it is truly located. Hindus describe divinity as Brahman, an all-pervasive Reality characterized as being (*sat*), consciousness (*chit*), and ananda (*bliss*). The blissful aspect of existence, Fry explains, may be accessed through meditation, a practice that requires no intercessor. In this way, she affirms, faith in God can blossom like a lotus flower, a natural process that unfolds and uplift's one life.

Robert Guyker, Jr., reflects on the immanence of the divine through an aesthetic sensibility. As a painter, he has imagined the divine to be a coming-forth impulse, a process of creative emergence. Since childhood he has seen the divine in the imagination. During his undergraduate studies, he turned within and sought an experience of the divine through prayer and meditation. He found what he was looking for, but tells us that it is something beyond concepts and the imagination. Although he does not identify himself as an adherent of a particular religion, he uses language that most closely resembles Buddhist and Taoist traditions. The divine is no-thing, an emptiness that is also an abiding presence; emptiness is not a vacuity, but a space within himself and others that he experiences through the warmth of silence, a still point that is the groundless ground of creativity. Guyker also focuses on the relationship between silence and the speech that arises from it in the form of stories or myths we tell ourselves. The stories, he argues, truly matter: "We get the God we deserve."

James Heaton reflects upon the religious impulse that is the source of both religion and science. Our knowledge-seeking nature and quest for discovery evoke the God complex: a constellation of feelings and ideas, often numinous, that awaken moments of cosmic beauty, as well as religious movements for justice and fairness. He feels that there may be no personal god that can save us from our difficulties, but affirms that there is an intelligence inherent in the cosmos to be found in the hidden half. Heaton agrees with Jung's and Edinger's contention that religion and the religious impulse have their roots in the transpersonal realm of the unconscious. The God-image, he adds, is constantly evolving in response to human needs and, presently, does so in a context of unprecedented religious pluralism. Heaton's own life is a case in point. He was raised in a family that engendered a dynamic tension between religion and science. As an avid reader, he delved into esoteric materials and was influenced by neopaganism and the Hermetic tradition, seeking a perspective that balanced the rational and the mythic, or the Apollonian and the Dionsyian, aspects of life. He found what had eluded him during a two-year cultural immersion in China and subsequent marriage into a Chinese family: a God-image that he characterizes in terms of balance, harmony of opposites, and comfort with paradox.

In his poetic musings, Gabriel Hilmar makes a passionate plea for a God-image characterized by love and beauty. He argues that the most influential forms of the Western religions have dissociated us from nature, precipitating the ecological crisis that threatens our survival. He turns to Taoism and mystical traditions for perspectives that can restore our connection to the cosmos that surrounds us and the nature within that is our soul. As a musician and a poet, he focuses on images and emotions that shift our perception and open our hearts—the Buddha's flower sermon, the depiction of the sacred heart of Jesus, the smile of a loved one—imploring us to experience life vividly as it unfolds in the present moment.

As a yoga teacher and new mother, Rachel Shakti Redding muses on the mystery of existence embodied by her daughter. The birth of her child, she tells us, deepened her contemplative sensibility and experience of love. Her own mother believed in the divinity of Jesus and the idea that God is love. Just as she received love from her mother, she transmits love and compassionate values to her daughter within the Hindu tradition she has come to embrace. Her *bhakti*-inflected version of Hinduism is pluralistic and affirms that religious experience is the living source of all traditions. Redding values Jung's concepts of individuation and wholeness, but not the Kantian epistemology that confines divinity to the God-images constructed by the psyche. For Redding, the divine is an independent being or beingness that pervades everything, what Hindus describe as Brahman, which is present, too, within the lotus of the human heart as the *atman*. This all-pervasive Reality is her transcendent God-image—something that can be *experienced*, she maintains, in the stillness of contemplation and meditation. Like her own mother, though from a Hindu rather than a Christian perspective, she affirms that the nature of this divinity is love.

Atheist and Secular Spirituality

The essays in this section represent different versions of atheist and secular spirituality, perspectives that are deeply informed by art, depth psychology, and science. Like Mark C. Taylor, each contributor offers a perspective that comes *after* God, that is, a response that reflects how we may understand spiritualty after the death of the traditional God-image in the context of secular culture. Some essayists write as atheists in the traditional sense as persons who deny the existence of a theistic deity. Others see the "death of God" as the basis for new ways of understanding the divine and non-traditional modes of spirituality.

Timothy Hall is deeply impressed by Mark C. Taylor's *After God*, appreciating it not only as insightful scholarship but as a work of art. As an artist, Hall focuses on Taylor's analysis of *figuring*, the way whereby meaning is constructed within a relational matrix of schemas for understanding existence. Hall discerns the trajectory of thought that informs Taylor's own schema, noting the way in which our cultural life entails *poiesis*. We make and shape our world through intentional actions and choices. However, Hall observes that our figuring is also deeply influenced by the archetypal structures delineated by Jung's depth psychology, a dimension that is given scant attention by Taylor. Hall's own stance may be described as an aesthetic spirituality that celebrates the world-making power of creativity as it arises from depths of the unconscious. The sacred abides, for him, not in a transcendent God but in the energy contained within the psyche.

In another essay that deeply appreciates *After God*, Daniel Ortiz finds that Taylor's analysis of religion as a complex, adaptive system that permeates culture needs to be supplemented by a depth psychological understanding of the emotional complexes that animate religion. He argues that James Hillman's concept of *pathologizing*—the psyche's autonomous ability to create illness, morbidity, disorder, and suffering—is also needed if we are to understand the dynamics of religions in culture and in our psychological life. Such phenomena are not diseases or problems to be conquered, but natural events that connect individuals and cultures to soul. Ortiz himself struggles with the tension between Eros and Thanatos, seeking to find a God-image that can address what he can theorize with what he can actually feel and live.

In an essay that muses on the paradoxes of quantum mechanics, John Redmond describes a God-image informed by the expanding cosmological worldview revealed by physics. He stresses the importance of moving out of the comfort zone of our inherited beliefs derived from Biblical religion and Newtonian science. He advocates for a secular spirituality that emerges from finding one's own way in a universe where God is literally neither here nor there. For Redmond, God connotes an inexhaustible mystery that inspires an attitude of wonder and discovery.

Reflecting on Friedrich Nietzsche's proclamation of the death of God, Haydeé Rovirosa observes that when God becomes silent, it means we have lost a shared myth or meaningful story that makes sense of our world and our place in it. For some, the silence of God may be the silence of absence and death; for others, it may be the silence of mystery and a new kind of presence. In Rovirosa's view, the death of God creates a clearing, an open space, in which something new can emerge. She is convinced that a new spiritual worldview is emerging around us in mysticism, science, psychology, feminism, and, most importantly for her, in art. The new vision of God emerging in our times is best characterized as poetics. Poetics brings forth what has been hidden and silent into presence, giving symbolic expression to a new *mythopoiesis* of God: a new vision of wholeness and a new sense of how we may relate to each other and the world. For Rovirosa, artists point the way; indeed, art *is* the way. As she puts it, "Art is not merely an aesthetic activity; it is, like philosophy and religion, a path and a way of being." The trauma of the death of God, she believes, may be overcome through the rebirth of God in new images. In this way, she affirms an aesthetic spirituality that engenders creative emergence in the context of the postmodern world.

Reflecting on her childhood, Angela Sells recalls two powerful impressions that have shaped her worldview. An anesthesia-induced vision of God provided feelings of warmth, love, and safety. The other impression came from learning about the Holocaust while reading *The Diary of Anne Frank*, an experience that led her to abandon religion completely. While she retains a nostalgic longing for the loving presence of the divine, she has spent her life trying to reconcile religion with the darker realities of humanity. Intellectually she aligns with the hermeneutics of suspicion, seeking to understand

and ameliorate the darkness that religion seems unable to effectively address. On the other hand, she distinguishes herself from the New Atheists such as Richard Dawkins who attack religion by maintaining that religion is the primary source of sexism, racism, and violence. Her more nuanced approach integrates C. G. Jung's insights regarding the paradoxical God-image of Judeo-Christian traditions, spirituality as an individual affair, and the Dalai Lama's observation that atheists (including Buddhists) affirm a humanism grounded in the principle of compassion. In this way, Sells articulates a genuine form of atheistic spirituality that transcends the polarized opposition between traditional believers and atheistic critics of religion.

The Holocaust has also deeply affected Odette Springer's spirituality. The death of six million Jews shattered both her mother's faith and her own. How God could have allowed such a thing was an unsolvable koan and the impetus for her subsequent spiritual journey. Springer migrated to Buddhism and Hinduism. Zen, in particular, provided an entry into her interior life as well as a Father archetype, which she describes as a powerful, yet stern, container for her symbolic life. When she recently discovered a list of one hundred forty family members who were gassed by the Nazis, her deep grief made her revisit her motives for discarding her Jewish heritage. She also began to deeply question other aspects of her spiritual journey: her attraction to Zen, the internalization of masculinist aspects of Hebrew mythology, and a lack of interest in the archetypal feminine and Goddess myths. Through examining and deconstructing the source of her indoctrination, she is revisioning her personal and inherited God-image. In Jungian terms, such self-inquiry is at the core of individuation. As an artist she privileges creativity above all else. Like Mark C. Taylor and fellow essayist Haydeé Rovirosa, she insists that the death of the traditional Western God-image gives way to the birth of the divine artist. As her journey continues, her touchstone is Jung's creed: "follow your libido wherever it takes you."

Raised as a Mormon in a conservative Christian home, Dane Styler has felt alienated by religion since childhood. The God he learned about in church was a foreign entity, an Other, though he had intimations that God was something that originated within himself. Decades later, he discovered that his thoughts about God and religion were anticipated by Lugwig Feuerbach and other nineteenth-century thinkers: God is a projection of human qualities we most admire, ideals such as goodness, truthfulness, love, wisdom, and strength of character. Styler's views are also influenced by the hermeneutics of suspicion and Jung's depth psychology. He asserts that the Christian God-image conceals a destructive nihilism. God—as Other—alienates us from ourselves and the natural world, and absolves us from our moral responsibilities. Accordingly, he asks: "What might the world be like without God?" Jung's influence, however, qualifies his atheism. The God-image also points to the numinous energy in the collective unconscious. Styler remains open to what God might be if we recognize this energy as intrinsic to our humanity.

Collectively the essays in this volume exemplify emerging forms of postmodern spirituality: diverse, highly personal configurations of beliefs, ultimate concerns, and practices for cultivating the inner life. Each is a powerful testament to the interdisciplinary study of myth, religion, and depth psychology as a means for revisioning one's understanding of the divine. May readers be inspired by these accounts of conscious individuation to engage in modes of spirituality that engender wholeness within and compassion for all sentient life.

PART I

Theistic and Monistic
Spirituality

CHAPTER 1

GOD AND ME AT SEVENTY-THREE

Julia Stone Berg

At the age of three, I became aware of my God-image. I was sitting on a little stool in our kitchen, witnessing my parent's battle escalate into a trip to the hospital emergency room. I was terribly frightened, but in my terror I suddenly knew that I was not totally alone. I didn't think about it, but I knew that the ultimate and only hiding place was what I now describe as being within God. I was severely punished when I told the doctor that the story my father had just told about my mother's injuries was not true. This pattern continued throughout the years of my parents' lives. My God-image was always a living presence and somehow strengthened me to hold the truth so that I could continue to survive in the reality of my home life.

As a child, I would have preferred to have someone with skin on, but as the years passed, I realized that my God-image was always with me in a way that no being with skin could ever possibly be. I called my God-image "God," never Jesus, mother or father. I was always quite certain that my God-image was not an invisible playmate or a guardian angel. I learned very early that my God-image was an immensity holding me as a tiny part. I did not find God; God found me.

At four, I started kindergarten in a private Catholic School and I was introduced to nuns with rulers and their version of God. I learned about ritual, rules, sin, saints, and an all-knowing, all-powerful God, quick to judge and punish. The binary system had entered my life. I now had "Church God" and "My God" and I knew they were not the same. I had no problem with this since my parents were one thing in public and entirely another at home. The two most beloved people in my life, my Great-Aunt and her brother, my Grandfather, represented two different sides of godness.

Great-Aunt Bess was an example of all that is good about Church God. She truly lived her Catholic faith and walked in loving-kindness. My Grandfather thought Church God was Grand Poobah, but guided me to expand My God into a universal God-image which could be seen in all of creation. The wind, the tiniest spider, the maize peeking up in the Spring, the intricacies of chemistry; the joy of music leaping to the soul, the special wisdom of poetry; and the beauty of human loving-kindness—all were the face of God. My God-image became much bigger and I belonged as a part of this "god-ness."

At ten, I discovered another connection between Church God and My God. A very compassionate nun, my piano teacher, gave in to my pleas and allowed me to learn to play the organ. She assigned another piano student to play the keyboard while I played the pedal board, since I was too short to play both. She allowed us to play in tandem for Mass until I grew barely tall enough to manage on my own. Liturgical music became another way for me to talk to My God. Church music was part of my God-image and part of my identity.

At thirteen, I wandered into the Chancellor's office of the Catholic Cathedral where I was organist. Monsignor Ignatius Strecker was Chancellor at that time and later became the first American Archbishop born in Kansas. He was an austere, dignified man, and more than a little intimidating. Nevertheless, I asked to see him and for the first of a great many times, he made room for me in his busy schedule. I instinctively knew I could trust this learned, mystical, compassionate man. He told me to stop praying for my parents and to accept that only their deaths would change them. My job was to grow up and follow my heart wherever it lead me. When I asked about the law of the church, he said, "You must always place following your heart and your conscience first." My God-image grew bigger because of this priest who saw beyond and within. In this good man, I found holiness with skin.

At twenty-one, my right thumb was severed in an accident. I was working on a Ph.D. in Music Performance. In an instant, what I had known as my life ended. When I was assured that I would never perform again, suicide was the only way I could see to end the excruciating pain and sense of loss. I was pronounced dead and went through what is now called a near-death experience. It was an experience that I kept hidden for many years and have never been able to describe. All sense of self was gone and yet I had never felt so myself. There was no thought as there were no words with which to think. It seems so inadequate to say that I was absorbed in love: there was no church God; there was only God, beyond imagination and indescribable.

When I eventually came back to consciousness in the hospital to find that I had survived, the disappointment was devastating. All I could think of was a quote from Corrie Ten Boom. She often spoke of her sister, Bessie, dying in Ravensbruck Concentration Camp, saying, "There is no pit so deep that God's love is not deeper still." That quote resonated with me then as it does now. Half a century after my near death experience, the living memory, a pale shadow of the reality, is there in meditation. Everything I thought I believed about God and religion was gone in that single instant, replaced by a deep knowing that has never left me. I lost all fear of death and will carry the intensity of Presence with me as long as I live.

For many years, I struggled to maintain a grip on religion. I left the Catholic Church and became an Episcopalian, after earnestly sampling many Christian churches. When I was fifty-one, I finally gave up and decided to stop trying to fit into organized religion. It was extremely painful at first, but I soon found that my God-image and I get on quite well together without a specific meeting place, uniforms, labels, or potluck suppers. I no longer search for a church home where I can belong. I am now free to belong anywhere and everywhere. Over the years, my God-image and I have become simpler through constant, careful editing based on my sense of love, truth, compassion, and authenticity.

I continue to find pieces of my God-image that need to be chiseled away. Pieces that have been chipped off include beliefs such as: My God will change my life circumstances to suit my preferences and My God will grant favors as an eternal Santa Claus might. Chipping away unwanted pieces has revealed that My God is not Catholic or Jewish or Buddhist or Hindu or American Indian, male or female. My God is none of them and all of them. My God-image allows me to imagine God as many, varied, and true, as mirrored in all of creation and universes, beyond number, description or thought. In my seventies, my God-image continues to grow with my heart and mind and soul and remains a constant presence with or without my willing acknowledgement, independent of joy or despair, and certainly in spite of my sense that I understand less and less as I accept more and more.

I believe that religion can be important for humankind. Released from its time-encrusted strait-jacket, it can serve our deep needs, just as training wheels on our first bicycle keep us upright and moving down the road and just as a raft keeps us from drowning and gets us to the other side of the river. Religion, freed to adapt to the "desperate darkness" (Edinger 61) of this century, can help us in our search for that infinite wholeness in which we are all connected (Taylor 356-357, 359). At its static worst, much of religion will continue to pit us against one another and rob our world of hope (348-349).

My values are sprinkled throughout this reflection paper, as are indications of my temperament (psychological type). It is probably evident that I am strongly introverted. In Enneagram typology, I am a "Four" (Daniels and Price 34). The Myers-Briggs Type Indicator shows that I am an INFP (introverted intuitive feeling perceiving type), and on V. Walter Odajnyk's Archetypal-Motivational Typology Scale (220-225), I am an Introverted Pneuma type and have tendencies toward Introverted Eros and Soulful temperament types.

My research interest in gender issues, especially in the often silent community of the transgendered, is based on the value I hold for the preciousness, unique identity, and connectedness of every living being. I believe that we are all of equal value and that any definition or label that diminishes any of us demeans and devalues us all.

CHAPTER 2

EVOLUTION OF THE WESTERN GOD-IMAGE

Susan Chaney

The Western God-image is continually evolving. From our perspective today, it is easy to look back and visually see how humanity's images have shifted and evolved. Some of the earliest God-images are depicted in cave paintings where humanity's Gods were animistic. Today's God-images are varied and are visible everywhere, from magazine ads selling products, through sexuality, to science seeking the "God particle." It is possible to see the movement of culture in societies through the images found in art and artifacts. Cultural movement also emerges in philosophy, literature, economics, and many other areas. As cultures merge and interact, images change and are infused with expanded meaning. Many of these early images portray humanity's understanding of its relationship to the divine. The foundation of the humanities even today is strongly influenced by religion. As human beings, we are continually creating an ordering process that explains one's relationship to the cosmos. It is an arrangement that provides balance within one's society.

If anyone has seen the night sky away from city lights, it is easy to imagine the sense of awe early humanity might have felt. Perhaps it is a feeling of being a small part of the whole universe. This relationship is revealed in the Greek word *kosmos*, which means whole. One begins to see the relationship of image and ordering of the self in the universe. As Mark C. Taylor, in *After God*, states, "Order and disorder are not simply opposite but are codependent in such a way that neither can be what it is apart from the other" (15). Chaos calls us to attention. We immediately want to make sense of it, give it meaning, and place it within a system of stability. But chaos is also part of creative emergence that erupts and shakes foundations. Taylor points out, "At the edge of chaos lurks not only danger but also the prospect of creative emergence, which harbor the only hope that still remains" (185). Chaos provides an opportunity to create new forms and expands one's worldview.

Whenever there is chaos and polarization, society is experiencing the paradox contained in the God-image. C. G. Jung believed that chaos in society was a manifestation of the collective psyche. The divine conflict contained within the paradoxical God is lived out collectively on the social plane (Edinger 112). Looking at the world today, one may see chaos erupting everywhere. Taylor explains that, "As connectivity spreads, complexity increases and, correlatively, instability and uncertainty grow" (3). Humanity is being barraged with many different kinds of information at a phenomenal speed, to a point where individual processing becomes difficult. We have instant access to images depicting destruction by natural disaster, protests, body image, and much more. While some images may be disparaging, there are images and information that create positive movement and inspire people to become involved. Information also allows a democratization of access to technology. Is this really so different from other eras such as Roman expansion, the Enlightenment, or the Industrial Revolution? Every shift in thought through connectivity creates a certain amount of instability.

The continued momentum pushes society through a birthing process, a reassembling of information. Some of the old ideas and images may remain, but they are merged with new ideas and images. Edward Edinger, in The New God-Image, explains that, "All God-images are modes of expression of humanity's experience and understanding of the autonomous psyche . . ." (xv). As humanity grows and develops, our God-images also grow and develop. One's images of religious reality originate from the archetypal psyche. C. G. Jung discovered that one's religious reality "derived from an inner, purposeful, non-ego origin" (Edinger 21). The new images hold an archetypal charge for the members of society. In this unprecedented technological revolution, images of God are becoming less rigid and more dynamic and, like the movement of fluid energy, can easily become new forms.

Whatever one's worldview, it is an expression of who one is. The way one dresses, the language one uses, and the way one moves all metaphorically reveal our self-understanding. By looking at the evolutionary sequence of the Western God-image—which Edinger describes as animistic, matriarchy, hierarchical polytheism, tribal monotheism, universal monotheism, and individuation—one can see the development of the psyche (xv). The psyche's structure is such that every experience is associated with meaning. As Edinger explains, C. G. Jung taught that one "cannot live a meaningless life" (30). When one begins to feel that life no longer has meaning, there is restlessness and a call to action, to change, and to find something that will bring meaning and significance back to life. These developmental stages happen individually, socially, and globally. The God-images represent the shifts and changes.

The images we have today may appear to be new, but they are built on the foundations of the past. Our thoughts emerge and regenerate around old ideas that trigger new ways of seeing the future. Taylor states that, "Though the past always conditions the present and influences the way in which the future is imagined, it is not fixed. To the contrary, the past is repeatedly refigured in light of the present and the anticipated future" (380). Form and structure are constantly influencing humanity's thought process.

While popular images today may depict consumerism, sexuality, and power, these images cut one off from one's own inner depth. They are superficial images, but are still an aspect of the God-image. These images trigger reactions within society. We see the polarization of fundamentalism and secularization. Secularization may appear to be the demise of religion, but as Taylor suggests, "Religion does not return, because it never goes away; to the contrary, religion haunts society, self, and culture even—perhaps especially—when it is absent" (132). While fundamentalism clings to absolutes and secularization seeks its answers in science, they both look for something more—a sense of wholeness.

Perhaps part of our spiral of self-destruction is our Newtonian, parts-based relation to self and the world, wherein "one discovers the logic of the facts of experience" (Taylor 92). In this view, the feelings and emotions of an experience are often ignored; only measurable parts are examined. When all the parts are examined, often one part becomes preferred over another. Preference creates division, incoherence occurs, and chaos erupts. Chaos is a call to examine what is erupting and to acknowledge those aspects of us that are screaming for attention, crying for wholeness and harmony. Humanity is calling for unity. All of our parts are essential, but within diversity creativity thrives. It is in the depths of our creativity that images are formed.

Duality is a part of our structure. Whole God-images carry this message. Individually and culturally, we continually collide into each other with seemingly different ideas. The Dalai Lama, in *Towards the True Kinship of Faiths: How the World's Religions Can Come Together*, states that religions are relevant for they have "inspired the flow of compassion and great acts of altruism . . . [but] the faith traditions must find a way of relating to each other with mutual acceptance and genuine respect" (xiii). Compassion and respect open the door to understanding. Compassion and respect subdue the ego. The clashing forces of difference are seen is a new light, where what is similar becomes the focus.

While many believe that our future will be found in science, science is also revealing that we are destroying ourselves. Yet, it is also showing us that we are creators. Through science we are able to cure disease, create limbs, and see stars beyond what the visible eye can detect. What we were not able to detect in the past is now becoming visible, tangible, and real. We are being called to our own divinity, but that divinity is a call to create responsibly with respect to all of humanity. We have the opportunity to create in tandem rather than in opposition.

CHAPTER 3

GOD:
MY IMAGINAL VIEW

D. Maggie Dowdy

When the day is clear and sunny, I look up and gaze, unfocused. The blue of the sky transforms into a kaleidoscope of iridescent dots, akin to an impressionist painting. Perhaps this is an illusion. Yet, the woman who showed me this trick explained that these dots are nothing more than the energy from which we are all made. In my early teens, I remember gazing up and wondering: Is this what God looks like?

Several years later, I still wonder. Yet, these days I reflect more upon how God is defined, rather than how S/He might appear. For if God could be seen, or conceptualized at all, I believe S/He might manifest at this impressionistic level of iridescence. Just as Moses hears the voice of God in a burning bush that is not consumed by the flames (Exod. 3.2), I imagine that any manifestation of the Divine will appear at an elemental level of human cognition. However paradoxical, I believe in the possibility of a transcendent intelligence that infuses the whole of what we can and cannot know, with a mystery and a purpose that is beyond our current comprehension.

Perhaps this is why, although his descriptions appear modern and technological, I am drawn to Mark C. Taylor's view of religion as an integral aspect of the complex network underlying today's Western culture. In fact, Taylor proposes that Protestantism particularly informs the "complex interrelation between religion and secularity" that is reflected in our globalized society today, especially "where it is least obvious" (3).

Although God is not specifically mentioned, His transcendence is implied in Taylor's argument for the Protestant influence. Yet, simultaneously, religion is viewed as an interconnected web, an "emergent, complex, adaptive network of symbols, myths, and rituals" (Taylor 12). Just as we might emerge from the undifferentiated substance of the iridescent energy seen on a sunny day, so our concepts of God continually reformulate in what Taylor refers to as a "quasi-dialectical rhythm" (13). This paradoxical image of an immanent transcendence is reflected in both the "ancient cosmogonic myths and modern information theory" (Taylor 14), and colors my God-complex as well.

My view of God, like Taylor's concept of religion's influence on society, has changed over time. As a child, if I imagined God at all, he appeared as a white-bearded old man, stern but remote. It was difficult to imagine that such a being could be everywhere at once. Yet, I was assured that He was everywhere, watching with stern disapproval every mistreatment of my sister. It was much easier to identify with Jesus as God's kindly son. Perhaps my opinions were colored by the patient nuns who introduced me to the parables of Jesus all those years ago. Those stories resonated with me, recalling my favorite tales from *Aesop's Fables*. Conflating the idea of Jesus, the Son of God, with God the Father, allowed for a sympathetic image that nourished my faith in the Roman Catholic Church.

However, discovering that Catholicism is just one of many paths in Christianity, and that Christianity is one of many kinds of faith, caused me to question its validity in defining the sacred. It was not God's existence that I questioned, only the religious dogma surrounding how S/He is defined.

As a young adult, when I thought about God at all, I wondered which belief-system might know the truth about God. By middle age, I doubted any faith professing absolute knowledge. After all, considering their differences, they cannot all lay claim to the ultimate truth. Like

Jung, I believe it to be impossible to truly "know God" (Jung qtd. in Edinger 124). We can only imagine and define such a concept within the limitations of our human imagination. This is what Jung refers to as an anthropomorphic God-image (Jung qtd. in Edinger 131). My doubt became outright mistrust of all religious institutions, and my conception of God devolved into something remote and indistinct.

Lately, my perspective shifts anew. Instead of dismissing all religion as misguided, I note aspects of truth, even when doctrinal beliefs clash. I no longer feel the need to seek an ultimate truth about God. Like the Dalai Lama, I see the futility in attempting to find the "ultimate oneness of all religions," embracing instead the differences in the various faith perspectives (148). Still, my God-complex defies concrete definition, tending more towards an embodied experience of amorphous energy. Yet, I also believe in the Divine potential to manifest in any imaginable form. My image of God continues to present as Divine energy, remote in its mystery out there, yet permeating and informing our very presences in the here and now.

CHAPTER 4

ENGAGING THE EROS DRIVE: TO BE IS TO BE CONNECTED

Daniel Gurska

Foundations

The worst thing my mother has ever experienced is the death of her first born child. The worst thing my father has ever experienced is attending the funeral of his first born child. There is a lot of space between those two things.

The worst thing my older brother has ever experienced is the violent hand of his father. I accidently set our microwave on fire at age seven, trying to cook something in a metal container. Our father came home and, furious at the sight of the charred appliance, grabbed my brother by the ear, lifted him from the ground, and smacked him square in the face. Our brother offered himself up as a shield countless times. He still does this, now for strangers, in his career as the head of security at the Mall of America. He is a warrior in the best sense.

My older sister was born three years after the twins—three years after our parents buried their first-born son. The worst thing my loving sister has ever experienced is cruel neglect from her parents. When she was eleven, she got her first period. We were home alone. Once she discovered the drops of blood, she screamed in terror. In a complete panic, we stuffed copious amounts of toilet paper in her underwear. My sister is now a nurse and is the very opposite of neglectful in everything she does. People often call my sister an angel and they are correct.

I am the youngest of the three surviving children. On a cold January day in Minnesota, the three of us were packed up and sent to our father's house for the weekend. His house didn't have running water, electricity, or heat. He and his new wife left us huddled around a kerosene heater while they went out for a special dinner. I knew it was wrong. All of us did. The next morning, they left the house again; this time they said they might not be back until the following morning. I called my mother to tell her about the situation and asked to be picked up. My mom pulled up in her Plymouth within an hour and honked twice. The worst thing I have ever experienced is the isolation I felt that day, when I popped out from under the shared blankets, grabbed my backpack, put on my boots, and saw my siblings, frozen. They were terrified to leave. They stayed. I cried. They cried. I couldn't convince them to leave. I was crushed. For the first time in my life I was completely alone. Anger filled me. I knew in that very moment that I permanently changed the family. I left and never returned to my father's house. I was eleven.

Memories

After our father left our mother, we were fed and clothed by the church. I think fondly of the church today, despite the hurtful whispers that echoed through her hallways. I never witnessed the gossip directly, but it had a large impact on us nonetheless. I toted a backpack that said, "Jesus is my friend" for years, before really knowing what it meant. It wasn't until our basic human needs as a family were adequately met— food, shelter, and a sense of belonging—that God and Jesus came into the picture. By that time, my family was in shambles. God seemed nothing more than a distant concept. I had no use for it.

When I was thirteen, my sister encouraged me to go to a Methodist summer camp. She went the year before and gained loads of fun stories and friends. I was an easy sell. An entire week away from the drama of home sounded too good to be true. My sister raised the money needed, lobbying for me by schmoozing rich folks who belonged to the church, so I didn't need to worry about a single thing. She truly is the best of our lot.

The six-hour bus ride up to camp was the highlight of my young life. I was in ecstasy. I acquired forty new friends instantly who showered me with smiles and hugs. Hugs are so damn powerful. We shared music, drawings, mad-libs, stories, and sugar-drenched snacks the entire ride up North. It was a scene I will never forget. I remember my sister smiling at me like a proud mother from the back of the bus. She knew I needed this; she needed it too. Three square meals a day, beautiful lakeside scenery, tons of friends to laugh and play with, music and song—we were in heaven! It was a tremendous gift to share it together.

A few days before bussing home there was a "Commitment Night," which was the crescendo of camp. The camp packed into the chapel for a special service once the sun dipped over the horizon and all tummies were sufficiently satiated. The pastor in charge gave a sermon unlike any other throughout the week. It was on opening your heart to Jesus and committing your life to him. I had no idea what the hell the pastor was talking about. Although our nose had been in scripture all week, I didn't recognize what the buzz was about. I wasn't moved by it. How could I commit my life to a character that lived a couple thousand years ago? What did committing my life entail? Was there a master switch inside of me to open my heart? I thought it comical. That was, until I looked around at my new friends and weeping sister. The chapel was full of sobbing children. The floors looked like they were sweating. The air became humid from the buckets of tears pouring out of the campers. Everything was hot and sticky and salty. I was uncomfortable. I felt alone again. I tried to get my sister to lock eyes with me, but she wouldn't look up. Her friends were holding her. I was envious.

The pastor invited those who wished to make the commitment to Christ to the altar. Many of my friends went forward. I watched in amazement as the pastor placed his palm on their heads, knelt down, and whispered gently to them. Their sobs then became hysterical. I started holding, hugging, and clutching every person near me. Their cries became contagious. Loneliness was ushered out of me by the tears. It was the most beautiful thing! We were openly vulnerable, personas tossed aside, and truly open to one another. People shared their most intimate confessions freely, without fear of judgment.

I was content standing on the sideline as a nurse for my fellow campers, but my sister wanted me to experience the altar. She peeled me away and led me to the altar while tightly squeezing my hand. We linked arms and bowed our heads in unison. By the time the pastor came over to us, the sides of our foreheads were pressed together. I was trembling. He took both of his hands and placed them on us. I don't remember exactly what he said. It doesn't matter. Loads of friends greeted us once we left the altar. They created a giant web of hugs and tenderness. I was completely overwhelmed. I never wanted to feel isolated again; the pastors told me I wouldn't, as long as I stuck to the Methodist plan. I was an easy sell.

Reflections

I share these narratives to express what is at the very heart of my God Complex. Although I have great distaste for the patriarchal sky deity that dominates the collective imagination, God—which I have come to regard as the unnamable, unfathomable, ungraspable mystery of life—is associated with warmth and connection. It isn't difficult, after hearing my stories, to understand why that may be. I discovered the divine through my connection with others. I delighted in making and recognizing the simplest of connections then, and still very much do now. This is why I have chosen to delve into mythological studies. Now I am never alone in my heroic victories or dire struggles; in a bizarre way, it feels as if I have amassed an arsenal, filled with characters from my studies, to defend my soul against loneliness. This makes sense according to my personality type. According to V. Walter Odajnyk's book *Archetype and Character*, I am an extroverted Eros type with inferior introverted power drive. Odajnyk writes, "Eros is an archetype whose principal aim is union—connections and relationships are the only means in which it pursues its goal" (44). This Eros drive within me is why the images and ideas surrounding the God archetype continue to be a source of deep gratification. Within each tradition explored, I have found common threads that connect back to fundamental teachings of love and compassion. As His Holiness the Dalai Lama asserts,

> On a metaphysical level, all major religions confront the same perennial questions: Who am I? Where do I come from? Where will I go after death? On the level of living a good life, all the faith traditions turn to compassion as a guiding principle. They use different words, invoke different images, root themselves in different concepts. But what they have in common is far more than what divides them, and their differences form the potential for a tremendously enriching dialogue, rooted in a marvelous diversity of experience and insight. (xiv)

Compassion, unity, plurality, relationship, diversity, integrity, and *harmony*—these are the ideas that surround the heart of my God complex.

CHAPTER 5

PAINTING:
EMBODIED PRAYER,
EMBODIED PRESENCE

Lynlee Lyckberg

My very first painting was of an image of God. I was five years old and I painted God as I imagined "Him" to be, which for me at that time was a little man in the sky. I remember feeling a deep sense of shame around this for some reason, probably because it generated so much interest and curiosity from my teacher. I lied to my parents about the nature of the image when asked, and told them that it was a picture of my brother going down the slide in the playground. This was my first memory of shame, combined with my first memory of a need to be secretive and covert around my beliefs in God.

Talking about how I envision God now is so much harder than I ever thought it would be. I intuitively know who and what I perceive that entity to be in my innermost self, and yet, I still cannot say out loud what God *is*. In a song written by Eric Bazilian of *The Hooters*, the question of who or what God might be is addressed in relationship to each of us as divine beings. Quite simply, Bazilian's song, recorded on the album *Relish* by rocker Joan Osborne asks, "What if God was one of us? Just a slob like one of us [. . .] Just a stranger on the bus, trying to find his way home" (Osborne). A slob like one of us? Surely God could never be a slob. Cleanliness *is* next to Godliness, after all. And yet, I am certain that God isn't anything like I have imagined.

Actually, I love this idea. What if God *is* one of us? The lowliest of us, climbing in the dumpster for a scrap of food because the game wasn't ever really rigged, and God subjected himself to human kindness as a kind of a test, and humanity just plain failed to recognize the Divine in this disguise? I think back to times when I was less than kind. Certainly I would have failed in my ability to care for the other, to feed the beggar, to see the Divine in everything and have gratitude for everything. The larger possibility exists that God is simply an energy field; a type of force field that is so much greater than I am; a matrix of possibility that has its own sense of organization and purpose that I am not really privy to; light taking embodied form through saturated color. The mystics believed this after all. I am not sure that I am smart enough to know the truth of these things. I suppose I could study physics just to learn a thing or two that could offer some kind of an explanation, but somehow the intelligence that animates the cosmic experience would still be way beyond me.

There are times when I believe that God is nothing more than the name we give to the unknowable universe, to the vast unknown that continues on and on and is beyond human comprehension. Not completely out of the question, in *The New God Image*, Edinger says that God must be described either anthropomorphically (as a human being) or mythically (26). Myth seems to work well for me in describing the unknown that I call God. I find the stories as good as anything else to describe what cannot really be known. Most times, I cannot hold the idea of God as an anthropomorphic Being. I claim that being is itself the expression of God. Most of the time, myths exist to point to something unknowable and not easily defined.

There are many things that have happened in life that make me question the God myth. Sometimes I find myself praying to an imagined power in the universe that I believe will protect me somehow if things get very difficult. I want to believe that something powerful and benevolent cares for me and loves me in a way that mere human beings cannot. Sometimes I encounter people who appear very godly and practice love in a very deep way. I try to embody that type of love, too, and offer it to others, because these people seem to know something that I do not. But somehow I fail in my attempts to be better, and I end up having to accept that I am a flawed human being. I must continually remind myself that I am just a beginner and that maybe another day I will be able to practice a type of self love and tenderness that is currently very hard to do.

Jung speaks of integrating the shadow, moving toward what is difficult, seeing self in others, and I struggle to be psychologically mature and on time in my efforts and actions. I rather like the psychological explanations of who and what God might be, and yet, I cannot relinquish my need to be deeply cared for by the imaginary beloved who goes by the name of God.

In the end, I have to admit that I don't know who or what God really is. Mark C. Taylor's definition of religion in *After God,* "an emergent complex adaptive network of symbols, myths, and rituals," is as good as any (12). It lends meaning to existence and simultaneously destroys all stabilizing structures.

When all is said and done, I return to the one activity that allows me to commune with my God, whomever or whatever that is. I paint because painting is my way of communing with the entity, power, or field that I like to call God, and somehow the very act of painting appeases my need to be doing something when I feel completely ineffectual and useless. It becomes my way of creating a visual prayer, a query or inquiry into the nature of the not yet known. As when I was five years old, I cannot cease from attempting to bring the unseen into form on the blank page, with a bit of paint.

Today I am content to accept what I do not know. I can allow God to remain a mystery, to allow even my fear of death, which I am convinced will bring me face to face with the divine mysteries, to remain an elusive intangible. According to the Myers-Briggs Type Indicator, based on Jung's theory of psychological types, I am an extroverted intuitive thinking type (ENTP) (Briggs and Myers 108-12). ENTP's are visionary beings that dislike routine and confining schedules. In light of the amorphous nature of the God-image, this typology makes complete sense for me. My aversion to anything concretized and static includes rigid ideas. ENTP's take the world in through intuition with thinking as a secondary mode. Our lives are process-oriented and we are most comfortable in fluid realms of consciousness. In *The New God-Image*, Edward Edinger asserts that the development of the God-image is not just a cultural process, but evolutionary and biological as well (xiii). The way in which we imagine our individual and collective divinity reflects a living dynamic process where we discover who and what we are. For Edinger, the ancient world was steeped in a consciousness of being that reflected the drama of the external universe, while modern humanity focuses upon the drama of the soul. These two dramas reflect the movement from consciousness projected outwardly to one focused on inner awareness and depth of being. Consciousness proceeds through successive stages, in a deepening process that contains the previous stage even as it moves beyond it.

The late French philosopher Maurice Merleau-Ponty believed that perception was an embodied experience rather than a thought process. His contention was that we perceive through our sensory experience long before we *think* about what that experience means. In this way, meaning follows experience, and we create meaning based upon pre-existing patterns and schema already established in our minds. There is an infinite possibility of experiences, but we can only experience a few. I send my silent prayers out for the things that I hope will come to pass, and I send my silent wishes of gratitude out for the blessings already bestowed. I hear God in the wind that rustles through the trees, and I see God in the faces of everyone around me. What if God is one of us? What if God is all of us? What if God is everything and no thing at the same paradoxical moment? Sometimes there are not definitive answers; I have learned to accept this.

CHAPTER 6

DIVINE EMANATION: REFLECTIONS OF A SPIRITUAL PLURALIST

Emmanuelle Patrice

After many years of education, intellectual intrigue, and a personal spiritual quest into other cultures and their religions, I now know that I have always been a religious pluralist and theosophist when it comes to religious and spiritual beliefs and principles. As children living under the roof of one's parents, our individuality and our innate faith or belief often undergo suppression. The Baptist denomination was my first taste of religion. I was quite ignorant of other religions as a child, with the exception of Catholicism, but even then I understood, or was taught, that Baptists and Catholics shared the same God. I never considered these faith traditions superior to any others, though as a child, my understanding of scripture was literal.

I first learned that God is Spirit from my Baptist upbringing and that He can enter or possess worshippers. Baptists referred to this phenomenon as "catching the Holy Ghost." As a child, there are no adequate words to express what one perceives when witnessing a person next to you or in the pew in front of you suddenly go into convulsions and fall to the floor or start speaking gibberish, which is referred to as *speaking in tongues*. In hindsight, it was quite a spectacle, because most of the time individuals caught the Holy Ghost during periods of song praise when the choir used tambourines, the organ, and drums to uplift the congregation. I recall watching my fellow church members go through their Holy Ghost experience and wondering how many more hours in church we had to endure. When my mom remarried into a Catholic family, the Mass was shorter in duration. Sadly, however, the experience of the transcendent Spirit touching or entering its worshippers faded from my perception and my spiritual core. Through the Catholic faith, I came to know that the only way to receive God's touch was to partake in the Eucharist, a symbolic ritual where one metaphorically absorbs the body and blood of Christ.

In the context of my subsequent studies, I concluded that religion was originally about spirituality—the spirituality of the individual. As individuals discover they share common spiritual beliefs and principles, religion becomes communal—a function of the community and eventually of the State. I now believe that religion is nothing more than a system of economic or social politics. Religion has become a system in which individuals with financial power, charming personalities, and savvy vernacular use their personal and spiritual beliefs to galvanize, manipulatively persuade, and control the naive or the ignorant.

From my viewpoint, religion has come to denote a dogmatic set of rituals, cosmology, and theology, embraced by individuals and communities as a means of explaining forces that supercede the laws of nature, human reasoning, and human control. Nevertheless, I agree with Taylor's gloss of Luther: "First and foremost, faith is a *personal* relationship between an *individual* self and the *individual* God. The relation, therefore, does not need to be mediated by the church hierarchy of pope, bishops, and priests but can be direct" (62). In this context, I have a renewed respect for the spirituality of the pagans and Wiccans. Pagans and Wiccans avoid exercising any forceful, authoritative, or extremist propaganda as a means of recruiting and converting other individuals. Instead, persons interested in the practices and teachings are invited to participate in rituals or discussions and left entirely free to decide for themselves whether they feel an affinity to the community or coven.

Rituals are performed for religious or spiritual objectives. They are essentially procedures or performances acted out as means of invoking and paying homage to God, the gods, divine beings, or our ancestors. Belief in cosmological, theological, psychological, or philosophical constructs influences perceptions, judgments, and actions. Belief and faith are the dogmatic constituents that comprise our spirituality as well as our religion. Spirituality, however, pertains to the wellness of the soul.

The term *God* is a name used to designate something beyond the limitations of human perception. God is not a being but a force, which I designate as Cause, an energy that is efficacious in all processes that animate the cosmos and the human psyche. It is also an acausal connecting principle that C. G. Jung refers to as *synchronicity*, a term that helps us understand the intricate correspondences between human and non-human reality. Cause is not exclusively male nor female, physical or psychological, visible or invisible. Rather, it transcends and includes such binaries. My God-image embodies the philosophies of animism (everything is alive), pantheism (the cosmos is divine), and panentheism (divinity both transcends and pervades the world). The image of divinity I embrace is the Cause of causes, the Thought behind thought, and the Spirit behind all substances. The image engenders a way of seeing and being that is expressed in the gnostic words of Jesus in The Gospel of Thomas: "I am the light that is over all things. I am all: From me all came forth, and to me all has reached. Split a piece of wood; I am there. Lift up the stone, and you will find me there" (55). Jesus's self-description conveys a God-image of the many as the myriad manifestations of the One—an emanation of the Godhead or Divine Spirit inherent in all forms of existence. This is the spirituality I affirm in a pluralistic world that urgently needs to behold the unity that underlies diversity.

Chapter 7

Postmodern Faith Without Relativism: Ethics Without Absolutes

April Rasmussen

> We are equal beings and the universe is our relations with each
> other. The universe is made of one kind of entity: each one is
> alive, each determines the course of his own existence. (Golas 54)

My dad remains the biggest influence on me when it comes to my
thoughts about God. He loves this little book by Thaddeus Golas
called *The Lazy Man's Guide to Enlightenment* and gives copies to
friends he deems worthy. My dad grew up in a very spiritual Roman
Catholic family and was taught by Jesuits in Brooklyn, but as soon
as he graduated, he hitchhiked to California with the clear purpose
of finding God. For a time, LSD was his path of choice and he still
credits it for much of his knowledge. Though I am quite active in a
very progressive Lutheran church and my pastor is still a dear friend,
it was always my dad who passionately wanted to make sure that my
spirituality was taken care of. His philosophy is firmly and simply
centered on the notion of love as the ruling order of the universe.
However, the foundation of his faith is not absolute, and beyond what
I have said, there is little that can be explained in any sort of clear
framework. My dad said that that was okay. There have also been
plenty of people who challenge this idea and challenge me to think that
there are absolutes that can be determined about God and everything.

My personal philosophy is a constant work in progress, as I assume is true for most other people. It usually comes down to the idea that absolutes might exist, but there is no way to get to them, and they are somewhat irrelevant because we live in a non-absolute sort of world. The point for me is to work with what you have and to love it all. Maybe love is my pseudo-absolute. Some people call me a relativist and maintain that nothing is meaningful without absolutes. The argument entails the dualism of what is versus what ought to be. Mark C. Taylor offers a comforting response. As he explains, "relativity does not involve a subjectivism that leads to nihilistic solipsism but entails a relationalism that draws everything and everybody out of isolation and into a condition of creative codependence" (356).

Taylor's chapter entitled "Ethics without Absolutes" caught my attention more than any other part of the class readings. It wasn't because he confronted the hypocrisy of the "culture of life" people, nor was it the clever use of water as an image as well as a quintessential global issue, although both of those topics are also important to me. He analyzes the worldview that is shaping most of the culture we see today, and also offers an alternative. I am so often disappointed by brilliant thinkers who insightfully articulate the problems that confront us, but fall short of proposing solutions. His views align closely with my own and relate to arguments I have with others pertaining to matters of faith and belief.

Consider the problem of absolutism as a case in point. It is the nature of faith to include doubt; it follows that faith cannot be absolute. However, absolutism is deeply embedded in the worldviews of many individuals and religious groups and, ironically, is associated with the notions of freedom and free will. Taylor describes how neofoundationalists view freedom: "autonomy is freedom *from* relationships rather than freedom *in* relationships" (350). This notion of freedom entails a denial of interconnectedness and it engenders a false sense of freedom; it is the quintessential American cowboy mythos. Freedom is associated with choice but, as Taylor observes, "choice degenerates in a consumerism that defines individuals by what they own" (350). However, quality of life isn't all about oneself or even one's insular circle of family, friends, culture or religion. Your choice is not entirely your own; it affects everything and everyone else. Taylor also critiques the related tendency to value competition over cooperation even with regard to concepts as personal as your body, ideas, and beliefs. Competition, coupled with absolute freedom of choice, demands that there be one winner and one right answer even to questions about ethics and our conceptions of God or the divine.

Remarkably, there is a historical remedy for this train of thought that comes from the Protestant Reformation. In relation to the absolutism dilemma, Martin Luther offered the following: "The private sphere should remain free from any regulation or outside intervention. As a result of human sin, however, the maintenance of civic order requires the regulation of the public sphere" (qtd in Taylor 351). There is lovely *both/and* language here, and a way to maintain a healthy relationship between the religious and secular spheres of life. It reminds me of a saying that actors use when playing improvisational games: the first rule of improvisation is that you cannot deny someone else's reality. An individual's beliefs and values belong to that person alone, whereas interacting with others requires support and a framework to operate within; in others, it needs a container.

My current study is asking what the container looks like today. The cooperative and unifying nature of love creates a specific and embracing space for mortals to interact and interrelate. As Luther suggested, the public sphere requires ground rules for how we ought to relate to each other, but there is not such an absolute requirement that defines what the outcome should be. The dynamic play of people's realities and emotions is the action within the container. The relational quality of life is the creative condition for making disparate pieces work together; it is the unifying force that binds us together—it is love. That love, for me, is God.

CHAPTER 8

TRANSCENDENCE AND IMMANENCE: A JUNIOR HIGH YOUTH GROUP LESSON

Elizabeth Wolterink

Yes, I am a Christian but don't run for the exits and don't tune me out, because I'm a liberal, far left, pluralistic Christian. I used to call myself a "weird Christian" until I discovered that there are more Christians like me than I thought. My inherited faith looks like a *Who's Who* of church history, so I appreciated Mark C. Taylor's exposition of the Reformation in *After God*. I have grandparents who are ministers in the Calvinist Dutch Reformed and Presbyterian churches. My mother was heavily influenced by both Greek Orthodoxy and the feminist spirituality movement. I was baptized in the United Church of Christ, a progressive social justice-oriented Church, and confirmed in the Lutheran Church (ELCA). I now teach in the Episcopal Church, the American form of the Church of England. All of these, as well as an early exposure to Native American religions, Zen, Hinduism, and a healthy dose of goddess spirituality influenced my teenage years and have informed the way I look at God and the phenomenon of religion.

Although I have chosen to follow the Christian path, my experiences have led me to a pluralistic view of religion, albeit slightly different from the Dalai Lama's views. In his book *Toward a True Kinship of Faiths*, the Dalai Lama rejects the metaphor of all religions as streams leading to the same ocean (147). However, because I do not believe that any one religion is the sole path to truth and because I am also a theist,

I have to believe that God is the mystery in all faiths. This does not mean that I think all religions are ultimately one faith or that every religion is just Christianity in disguise; nor is my personal religion necessarily the ocean all faith streams are flowing toward. It is not a paradox to me that all religions come from God and yet, as the Dalai Lama emphasizes, each religion really is different and unique from other religions (132). This conviction carries over into my teaching.

As a Director of Youth Ministries in the Episcopal Church for two years, I oversaw the religious education of children from kindergarten through twelfth grade. For the last seven years, I have been personally responsible for teaching junior high and high school students. Because I am consistently engaged with youth who are in the formative stages of building a faith amidst the culture wars, and because the way I teach reflects my own beliefs, the two areas which have resonated most with me from our readings are religious pluralism and the metaphysics of God and creation. When I slip the concept of pluralism into my classes, it must be within a particular context from the standpoint of a comparison with Christianity. While some of it may sound like appropriation, it is really an attempt at exposing students to other traditions. I try hard to make it clear that we are not conflating religions. Outlining one major theme from my class might give you an idea of both my pluralism and my Christian theology.

In the last few weeks I have been exposing my students to Trinitarian theology through a discussion of immanence and transcendence. My take on these two modes of theistic being differs from Taylor's analysis of the matter. Taylor takes the view that transcendence and immanence are mutually exclusive. For him, "transcendence shatters monism" or immanence (133). He suggests that the alternative to these two schemas is "neither/nor" (38, 40). The view I take, however, is panentheistic, with a dyophysite acknowledgement of the incarnation (a theology symbolized by the hand gesture used to cross oneself—pads of the forefinger, middle finger, and thumb touching represent the Trinity, while the bent ring and pinky fingers represent Christ's two natures— fully human and fully divine). What this means is that one God encompasses all three modes of being: transcendent, immanent, and incarnate. The Christian Trinity consists of the Father, Son, and Holy

Spirit (although I prefer to substitute "Parent" for "Father"). The Parent is transcendent, both male and female, and neither; beyond form, beyond creation, and beyond human conception or categorization. The Holy Spirit is immanent in the created universe: God the Holy Spirit is in, under, and through all matter, energies, and forces, and it is feminine. The Son is incarnate: God made flesh in the world (or as I tell my students to help them remember—*in carne*—in the meat). The Son is the masculine Jesus; God Transcendent is the ever-pregnant possibility; God Immanent is the vehicle; and God Incarnate is the emergent. I have discovered that these views are similar to Alfred North Whitehead's process philosophy and to process theology, although I had never been aware of these schools of thought until taking the seminar on the God complex (Mahaffey).

Conceptually, transcendence brings to mind Taoism and the first chapter of the *Tao Te Ching*: "The Tao that can be spoken is not the eternal Tao/ The name that can be named is not the eternal name . . . The unity is said to be the mystery/ Mystery of mysteries, the door to all wonders" (Lao Tzu). While the Tao is also immanent, it seems to help the kids more readily understand transcendence. I often refer to Hinduism to talk about both immanence and incarnation. Like Shakti, the creative feminine energy without which Shiva cannot act or reveal himself (Daniélou 76), the immanent Holy Spirit is the way God acts in the world. When we get to the incarnation I often bring up Krishna and the concept of avatars. Like Jesus, Krishna is divine. He knows it and those around him know it. Yet, he had a human birth and a human death, so in some ways, while not entirely theologically correct according to Hinduism, Krishna, like Jesus, may be said to have a dyophisite nature. Strangely, however, sixth through eighth graders seem to have far less trouble reconciling Jesus' two natures than generations of church fathers did, so I have never actually used this explanation to illustrate the "fully God, fully human" concept. The theme of incarnation is also where I reference Mary, and this opens the door for exposure to both Surah 19 of the Koran and to goddess spirituality.

Having introduced the metaphysics of the Trinity, I now move to the metaphysics of my students' existential nature. Christians believe that humans are made in *the image of God*. Rather than resulting in an anthropomorphic god, the Trinitarian theology I have outlined allows us to recognize the same modes of Divine being mirrored in humanity. Applying Trinitarian concepts to the individual human being also helps students to understand the "three in one" premise. You may also recognize shades of the Hindu concepts of *Chit* (Consciousness), *Sat* (Being), and *Ananda* (Bliss) in this.

Before hearing the Gospel, Catholics and Anglicans cross or touch their foreheads, lips, and heart, meaning "God be in my head, God be on my lips, and God be in my heart." These three loci correspond to the third eye, throat, and heart chakras of perception, expression, and emotion. This symbolic blessing can also be seen to refer to the tripartite natures of human being, action, and experience. Human beings are comprised of mind, body, and spirit that can be said to be our transcendent, incarnate, and immanent natures. The mind transcends corporeal reality, the body is subjective existence incarnate, and the spirit (*pneuma* or breath of God) is immanent in the body. Human action is also given a tripartite structure. *Thought* is transcendent possibility and *word* or *logos* is the immanent vehicle through which *deed* becomes incarnate realization. Our experiential natures (categorized as typologies by Jung) also reflect the Trinity: our feelings and sensations, experienced through and in the incarnate body; the intellect, capable of transcendent meta-thinking; and our intuition, pervasive and immanently present if we are open and listen.

All of this may appear to be interesting but useless speculation; however, belief in this kind of triune God and triune humanity can have deep and affecting practical implications. If God is immanent in everyone and everything, including ourselves, then, as Taylor points out, everything is sacred (133). (He goes on to say that if everything is sacred, nothing is sacred, but I do not agree.) If everything is sacred, then the cosmos, the earth, and other living beings, human and animal, must all be treated with care, respect, and compassion. Discussing immanence with my students invariably leads to questions of good and evil among humans, animals, and the earth, a topic that lends itself to Native American or Shinto perspectives. In conjunction with this immanence, God's transcendence presents us with the contradiction of our own subjectivity in veiled unity—a condition that also gives us free will. Our own transcendent capabilities provide us with another paradox: that of cognition—both concrete reason and the drive to conceptualize the unfathomable. As incarnate creatures, we are the hands and feet of God in the world and thus become co-creators, using our own transcendent and immanent natures to engage in what Taylor might call mimetic emergent creativity (111, 128).

While this is my current interpretation and what I present in my classes, I do not believe it is my job to tell my students what to believe. Rather, as a religious educator I feel that it is my responsibility not only to educate my students about the faith they were born into, but also to open their eyes to other spiritual paths, to help them learn about the world, and to encourage them to speculate about the nature of reality. Because I have been spiritually moved and enriched by other faiths and feel wonder at creation and awe at the mystery of God, I want to allow my students the same opportunity. I find religious exclusivism abhorrent and the denial of reason and quashing of questions equally so. I encourage my students to doubt and question, but also to trust themselves and God. I have found that doubt can build faith and questions lead to a deepening appreciation of the wonders, complexities, and paradoxes of the Divine.

PART II

THE DIVINE FEMININE AND GODDESS SPIRITUALITY

CHAPTER 9

TRACING THE
DIVINE LINES OF MY SOUL:
MOVEMENTS TOWARD WHOLENESS

Alexandra Dragin

The divine has been a constant mysterious presence in my life from the very beginning. The lines of the divine have run through my soul like converging paths in a shady wood or branching rivers flowing toward the sea; it has always seemed that feeling and knowing the divine would help me to fulfill my destiny. If asked whether I believe in God, I would echo Jung in saying, "I don't need to believe, I know" (27). My relationship to the divine may be expressed in spiral-like movements toward and away from this numinous presence, but always marked by transformations in emotional consciousness. Like Edward F. Edinger's stages of the evolution of the Western God-image, my own images of the divine have evolved, thereby teaching me how to love more openly and deeply.

Walter Otto once said, "At the beginning stands always the god" (qtd. in Cowan 14). As a very young child, I was taught that God was good and powerful, the loving, benevolent father and creator of all that exists. Raised in the Christian tradition of Eastern Orthodoxy, I have vivid memories of attending church every Sunday, which gave me an important sense of belonging to a spiritual community. What moved me most, though, were those elements of the experience that blended the sacred and the sensual. Despite complaining about waking up too early and having to wear my fancy clothes and sit quietly through a lengthy service that I did not understand, I knew when I stepped across the threshold that I was entering a sacred space.

I was met with a dim, hushed silence, small golden candles in sand trays brightly proclaiming prayers for both the living and the dead; beautifully rendered icons of the Virgin Mary, Jesus, and the saints, all glancing at me with sad, profound eyes waiting to be kissed; the sweet, heady fragrance of frankincense, the dark, hard wooden pews, light streaming through tall stained-glass windows, dancing in myriad colors on the floors; the beautiful, glorious harmonies of the choir echoing all the way to the very top of the church's central sun-lit dome, the ringing of the bells; the savory taste of home-baked bread; and finally, the sacred altar protected by several gilded doors through which the altar boys and the priest emerged. It was an extraordinary place, for God was there.

Everyone adored our priest. With his dark, handsome features, deep melodious voice, and his earthy charm and humor, he held the congregation in the palm of his hand. For my child self, the image of this man somehow became conflated with God, and when I prayed, I heard his comforting voice in response. I did not understand until much later why he was forced to resign, nor why he was replaced with a misogynistic, racist, ignorant man who literally made my skin crawl. Political maneuvering by other patriarchs hungry for power and position exposed the "scandal" of our beloved priest. He had been having an affair with another woman, who was rumored to be his first love. He was defrocked, divorced his first wife, and eventually married his first love. No one could explain why our strong, loving priest would not be forgiven. Wasn't that one of the central tenets of Christianity? He had sinned and that was the end of it—he was gone.

By then I was an adolescent and thoroughly confused about the strange morals perpetuated by our church. I began asking my own questions: Why weren't female children allowed to go behind the altar? Why did parishioners smile and kiss one another three times and then say nasty things behind each others' backs? Why were the many educated, caring women relegated to volunteering in the kitchen and fundraising instead of sharing in the leadership of the church? Why were those who suffered most, people who committed suicide or unbaptized children who died, not allowed to be buried in our graveyards and denied entrance to heaven? Why was everyone who wasn't a part of our Eastern Orthodox Church or Christianity doomed to hell? Why was the only acceptable image of a woman by the church a virginal mother?

I intuitively knew that I would not receive any insightful answers to these questions, nor would any of these dogmatic rules change, because it was what Mark C. Taylor would call a closed system. I needed a new paradigm, a new image, one that would provide enough new space to grow into and traverse. "Old maps cannot provide adequate guidance for new territories," explains Taylor (348). My soul began searching for new images and new paths, and she found them in my undergraduate studies in art, literature, and myth.

Fascinating new worlds opened wide when I was not only given permission, but encouraged to read religious stories or myths symbolically. More importantly, I encountered spectacular images of the divine feminine—Aphrodite, revered for her beauty and sexuality; Athena, honored for her wisdom and physical prowess in war; and Demeter, so powerful that she could cause the earth to yield a fruitful abundance or wither and die. I realized that these stories were perhaps more real to me than the biblical stories I heard repeatedly in Sunday school that were presented so literally and didactically. The possibilities for who I could be broadened and deepened in my reflection upon the goddesses; so many of those varied goddess qualities that seemed to be repressed, negated or simply omitted in my Christian background were celebrated and honored in myth. It was quite a revelation to study the comparative mythology of Joseph Campbell and to learn of other, more ancient mythologies whose creation myths included a powerful feminine presence, and from which Christianity borrowed many of its symbols and stories.

Encountering the goddesses and studying sacred narratives from a mythic, psychological perspective was liberating and evocative. These new, yet curiously familiar perceptions of the divine, felt more truthful. Now I did not feel ashamed for knowing that divine presence existed in other places besides the church—I could feel it in natural landscapes, when reading a beautiful poem, in the pain of loss and death, in intense emotional relationships between people, and even within my own heart. The powerful images of the goddesses helped me to leave a long-lasting abusive relationship, to cultivate my intellect through graduate study, and to trust in my own abilities to teach others.

I have not, however, abandoned my religion or my previous masculine God-image; rather, they all seem to co-exist in my psyche. I realize that Eastern Orthodoxy, despite its tendencies toward absolutism, has served my ancestors for centuries, acting as a lifeline during the darkest times. The church helped to preserve culture, history, language, and, perhaps most importantly, hope, during long stretches of occupation, war, and Communism. Yet, I can also see how the dualistic, dogmatic thought that is inherent in any orthodoxy can be both alienating and self-destructive. Taylor elucidates,

> To negate the other without whom one cannot be what one is, is to negate oneself. Nothing is more dangerous today than the growing devotion to dualistic either/or ideologies in a neither/nor world. If disaster is to be avoided, there must be a radical transvaluation of values that both reflects global complexity and promotes an ethic of life. (349)

As Taylor illustrates, all of the religions of today must find ways to promote a relational, compassionate stance toward others if we wish to survive.

Indispensible to this aim is Jung's concept of the objective psyche, which has helped me to understand the ways individuals and cultures anthropomorphize the divine. When many of us speak of God or the divine, what we are really speaking of are God-images, subjective or cultural ways of understanding that numinous force. Jung explains,

> My human limitation does not permit me to assert that I know God, hence I cannot but regard all assertions about God as relative because subjectively conditioned—and this out of respect for my brothers [and sisters], whose other conceptions

and beliefs have as much to justify them as mine. (qtd. in Edinger 9-10)

In other words, the divine is an ultimate mystery, utterly ineffable, except for the glimpses we may receive during our deepest experiences.

I conclude with a third image of the divine that engages my soul today—that of bittersweet Eros and the sacred marriage. I love Marion Woodman's conception of the divine as a marriage of the spirit (masculine, light, air) with the soul (feminine, dark, earth). In this vision, transcendence and immanence are complementary rather than in conflict with one another, and both are necessary to the flourishing of life. This image of the divine is an image of pure love, in which the divine masculine and divine feminine are two halves of a terrifyingly beautiful whole who serve one another in compassion.

CHAPTER 10

AN OFFERING:
A REFLECTION ON MY
CONNECTION TO THE DIVINE

Clara Oropeza

Reading Mark C. Taylor's book *After God* and reflecting on its overarching premise has helped me to better articulate my personal myth about spirituality. Taylor writes, "Religion is not limited to what occurs in churches, synagogues, mosques, and temples; rather, there is a religious dimension to all culture" (3). Taylor believes that it is "imperative to develop a better understanding of what religion is and how it functions" (4). While he is calling for a critical study of religion and its function in society, Taylor also believes that in order to have constructive dialogue, resistance to opposing views needs to be investigated. It is also "precisely this resistance that underscores the urgent need for renewed critical analysis" (4). Taylor's position reminds me, however, that an ability and willingness to have this conversation with oneself, first through reflection, must precede our ability to have this discussion in a larger context as a collective.

Thus, my reflection begins with the religious dimension of the Mexican culture I was steeped in as a child. I grew up around lit candles bearing religious images and saints such as the crucified Jesus, the Virgin de Guadalupe, and Saint Martin. Then there were the religious iconic images framed and displayed all around the ornate walls of the furniture-filled rooms in my relatives' homes. I witnessed with awe adults making the sign of the cross each time he or she walked past each frame. I observed my grandmother's ardent celebration of Dia de la Virgen De Guadalupe, the anniversary of the apparition of the Virgin de Guadalupe to Juan Diego on December 12, 1531. To most Mexicans, the Virgin de Guadalupe is a powerful national symbol of liberation, motherly protection and love, and—in a symbolic sense—a mother Goddess who embraces cyclical patterns. My grandmother saw the Virgin de Guadalupe as an embodiment of divine love. There were also the altars bearing images of recently deceased relatives surrounded by burning candles. I walked around these spaces mesmerized and awed to be a witness to mystery.

It is unsurprising that I concede that it was my Mexican culture that taught me the power of prayer, of connection to divine spirits. Throughout the years, the connection to evoking the divine in the ways that I saw my grandmother and other relatives engage in daily life gradually surrounded the God-image of Sunday mass. And when the God image presented at Sunday mass at times seemed distant, I knew I could rely on the other images my grandmother had on her altar. The empty feeling evoked by the God image of Sunday mass left me hungry for the feminine divinity to whom I thought my grandmother so ardently, in a soft voice, prayed. It is no wonder that in my adult life, psyche would continue this search as part of the work that today feels more like a calling to the Divine Goddess in efforts to engage a sacred marriage of the divine feminine and divine masculine.

The God-image of my Catholic upbringing somewhat faded from my life in early adulthood, and what stayed was a connection to spirit, to mystery, all leading to my spiritual life today. What is present in my life now is a deep desire to evoke, to *be* in the presence of, and to be *with* all that is divine. It is a longing for an active relationship with something greater than us. Today my spiritual practices draw from insights from indigenous spiritual traditions, practice in qigong, yoga, and vipassana meditation, long walks in nature with Emma, my dog, as well as in my writing. I now deeply know that there is a multifarious approach to prayer, and that the divine has many faces.

My path eventually intersected with the discourse of second and third wave feminist spirituality and the non-patriarchal narratives and ways of thinking that today feed my understanding of the divine. It was this call for divine feminine images that I hoped would help to infuse psychic imagination and to balance the one-sided concentration of divine masculinity. It has been this search for the marriage of the divine feminine and masculine that today infuses my work as a student, teacher, writer, and woman on a quest towards wholeness.

It is fair to say that my struggle to find my voice as a writer has led me to feminist thinking, to connecting with goddess mythology. I am drawn to the spirituality found in the poetics of literature, for reading many of my favorite literary works is akin to a religious experience for me, as is writing. As I pray and meditate on the subject of my dissertation, I have felt compelled over and over to write on the work of Anais Nin. The nature of my feeling that this is a calling is difficult to explain. I can't help but wonder if this is indeed what it means to be called by the unseen energy of divine grace. When I need to pray for flow and focus in my work, I find myself evoking Saraswati, and a prayer to her hums in my heart, and through a soft throat chakra, in the air: "May Goddess Sarasvati, who is fair like the jasmine-colored moon, and whose pure white garland is like frosty dew drops; who is adorned in radiant white attire, protect me. May you fully remove my lethargy, sluggishness and ignorance." I find that if I tend and meditate on these words, a commitment to writing is graced upon me. It is in this sacred space that I hope my writing will create a context for healing not only in my life, but also in the lives of others. I see my work fitting into a greater need in our culture for re-creating and integrating all that is divine in our lives, especially the ways in which the divine feminine and divine masculine are constellated. I am starting to connect to my emerging voice in my work as a rebirth. And when fear of not knowing what this voice yearns to express gets overwhelming, I am reminded of Marion Woodman's words that "Goddess energy can pull one from death to a creative living energy" (Woodman).

I experience my spiritual practices as answering a call not to a specific religion or away from religion. I see myself on a path towards reclaiming a personal relationship with the Divine. And it so happens that it is the same path towards finding my own voice. Today, the connection to spirit that I seek, and that seeks me, includes a connection to how I treat the earth and how I see my embodied-self within the context of all non-human nature. It is from this place of better understanding "what religion is and how it functions" in my personal myth that I hope to be bi-lingual, for it is through this form of bilingualism that I can join the greater conversation about opposing religious views that Taylor is asking us to engage.

CHAPTER 11

FROM GOD COMPLEX TO COMPLEX GOD/DESS(ES): MY GAIAN COSMOLOGY

April Heaslip

Once upon a time—just the other day—in another graduate school, in a distant land, a classmate of mine—who happened to be a Christian minister—asked me, late one night as we were talking about our spirituality, "Exactly what *do* you believe?" I paused and was surprised at how much energy it was taking me to reach deep inside to articulate an answer. Though I had been identifying as a pagan and a witch for several years, this was my first attempt at defining and simultaneously describing my worldview. As I reflect upon what I told her then and on the development of my cosmology since, I see three major events punctuating my trajectory.

Women's Circles

My spiritual path shifted dramatically twenty years ago when the week my mother died I came upon a poster affixed to a park tree in an oddly remote area that read: Women's Circle Forming. Relocating to Pennsylvania from San Francisco, a woman was offering a container for meeting on each new and full moon. I went. The group sometimes swelled to twenty-five or thirty women for seasonal events such as the summer solstice, and settled into eleven or thirteen as our core bi-weekly group. Together we found community and a chance to explore together, offering teachings we each felt proficient in or curious about. Leadership rotated among us for each circle as we taught each other drumming, the *I Ching*, songs and chants, how to use our hands for healing, mask-making, and stories of goddesses and gods. We built a sukkah for the Jewish harvest festival, May poles for Beltane, yule logs for winter solstice, and we lit hundreds of candles to celebrate the returning light.

Being with these women gave me a new psycho-spiritual purchase. I began devouring books on feminist spirituality, archaeomythology, shamanism, and pagan studies. These adventures coincided with the return to complete my undergraduate degree and influenced my shift towards women's studies and coursework in spirituality and its relationship to creativity. I studied the sociology of women's spirituality, filming a documentary on this new social movement, tracking women who left Jewish and Christian traditions to co-create something new, as well as those who were staying within these institutions in order to affect change from within.

It was from this place that I ended up heading north for graduate school in ecofeminism and sustainability and found myself having a conversation about my beliefs. This graduate program was founded on the principles of anarchy, embedded within an interdisciplinary model called social ecology. In my experience, pagans, witches, and other *people of the land* tend to feel quite comfortable with—or even seem to need—anarchist self-organizing structures and the potentialities inherent in such guiding principles. They tend to thrive where there is room for chaos theory, right relationship, and a sense of personal agency. So when Nancy, a petite and powerful minister from Texas, asked me what I believed, these ideas are what I came up with and have been tinkering with ever since:

> I knew I believed in goddesses and gods and their relationships
> with each other, the world, and me. But I did not understand
> what that meant to me or how to describe it.

I realized that discovering my true beliefs required a process of elimination; there were several things in which I decidedly *did not* believe. For example, other than a physical place on the map of Greece, I did not believe in Mt. Olympus as a gathering place for the Greek pantheon.

I had had direct and strange encounters with "deities," such as sightings and conversations. I had even received blessings from them. Yet, I could not identify them as something separate from *my* experiences, *my* psyche.

Instead, I came up with a flexible idea: perhaps gods, goddesses, and pantheons are how the universe organizes and continually reorganizes itself, to show us truths, challenges, and choices in life. Perhaps this was the language of divinity, of life itself.

I also believe in ongoing relationships with our ancestors, but not because I believe they congregated somewhere above, watching over us. Rather, I trust in the conservation of consciousness, and feel their presence after death in an integral, coherent, and oddly effective way.

I believe all land is sacred. It is only where we have desecrated it and forgotten how to tend it that we see the wounding results of our ways. One of my most sacred spiritual duties, along with cultivating relentless compassion for others, is to be in relationship with the land and to support her health, not only as integral to my own well-being, but for life itself.

Witch Camp

These perspectives were further shaped by the second major component in my cosmology: Witch Camp. This is where I received a crash course in *applied* Jungian and archetypal psychology that deeply informed my spiritual scaffolding. It was 1999 when I attended Vermont Witch Camp for the first time and subsequently became involved in Reclaiming, an ecofeminist, Goddess-centered pagan community that began as a collective in the San Francisco Bay area over thirty years ago. With teachings offered through local and online classes and publications, Reclaiming has created approximately seventeen international, weeklong and annual intensives for adults, teens, and families, known as Witch Camps. Attracting a wide range of participants, including therapists, scholars, artists, yogis and yoginis, political activists, and healers, the group has at its core a commitment to uniting spirituality and activism. Notoriously anarchistic, Reclaiming witches self-define and worship with diverse styles. At any given camp, you may find a fusion of horizons where *double-belonging* (belonging to more than one tradition) is the norm. These folks might self-identify as witches or vehemently not. Gender identity also contributes to the conversation. I invited my camp community to contribute how they personally self-identify and their responses included: feminist Goddess worshiper, pagan Quaker, atheist witch, queer priestess, slacker pagan who likes to be naked a lot, Jewitch, panentheistic pagan tree-hugger or priest, Buddhist yogini, Wild Woman, and cackling crone.

Each camp chooses a myth or theme for the year, such as Communitas or The Great Turning. Most communities work with traditional mythologies and sometimes utilize exciting and contemporary myths that have structural integrity and are often re-imaginings of older stories, like Baba Yaga, Avalon, the Descent of Inanna, the Wizard of Oz, Brigid, Amaterasu, Alice in Wonderland, La Llorona, Isis, Krishna and the Gopis, and Odin and the Runes.

By working within a mythic framework, facilitators craft an arc of rituals for the week, guiding the community through psychological and pedagogical stages of development while attending to the particular myth chosen and developed over as long a period as six months. Divination tools are used for planning by organizers and facilitators to tap into the group's collective unconscious. Meetings, whether online, via telephone, or in person, are always held in sacred space and begin with a form of meditation. How often I have wished that all groups utilized these very simple tools, for I have seen tremendous results.

Our co-created rituals and community norms embody key elements of depth psychology. Some of our founding mothers, including Starhawk, perhaps Reclaiming's most well-known author and co-founder, were trained together as psychotherapists and healers. We work with shadow, dream interpretation, active imagination, amplification, inflation/deflation, archetypal analysis, the descent to the underworld, and the s/hero's journey. Co-created rituals are designed to leave space for the collective unconscious to come through. Reclaiming-style rituals do not operate with standard liturgy, rather, they are improvisational, ecstatic, and embodied. We plan beginnings, endings, transitions and certain components of each ritual (such as drumming, choreographed dancing, and chanting), yet most are designed with the intention of moving into liminal space, allowing for spontaneity in play, storytelling, and movement in response to what comes up through the collective.

Liturgies and rituals are intentionally structured to support personal and collective healing and development; they are never designed to re-enact any previous or existing ritual, either in format or in content. Instead, they are freshly informed by a living tradition that consciously remains open and committed to the plurality of global mythologies and the needs of the community in the present moment. There is also a respectful and growing desire to work with indigenous traditions in solidarity and through activism in a manner that gives back to the land and peoples through whom these stories have arisen. As an example, I was on a teaching team that worked with the myth of Krishna and the Gopis and may have been the only attendee of that particular camp who was partially of Indian descent. I was deeply touched by how reverently the story was treated and honored for both its Hindu heritage and universality; I was also inspired to take a more direct and hands-on approach with activism for girls and women in India, the land where my beloved grandmother was born more than a century ago. I believe such cross-fertilization is profoundly effective for healing projection and suffering on many levels. The core components of this planning are the inclusion of indigenous leaders, a willingness to listen, and applied activism. My belief in our ability to heal ourselves, our communities, and the Earth has grown directly from this practice.

Archetypes as Sacred

Lastly, it was at Pacifica Graduate Institute where I discovered a strong congruity between Jung's definition of archetypes and my own cosmology. In a recent conversation with a dear friend, anthropologist, and practicing priestess from another tradition—who, by her definition, believes in a "literal" goddess—she suddenly and jokingly exclaimed: "I can't believe I am hanging out with an archetypalist!" For her, this term was derogatory and devoid of spirituality. However, as Keiron Le Grice explains in *The Archetypal Cosmos*:

> The archetypes were conceived by Jung as principles that are both instinctual and spiritual, both natural and transcendent. Indeed, such is the complex character of the archetypes that Jung felt it necessary to employ a wide variety of terms to describe them: gods, patterns of behavior, conditioning factors, primordial images, unconscious dominants, organizing forms, formative principles, instinctual powers, dynamisms—to give but a few examples. He suggests, furthermore, that the archetypes are "active, living dispositions, ideas in the Platonic sense, that preform and continually influence our thoughts, feelings, and actions." Jung therefore situates his theory of archetypes firmly in the mythic-Platonic tradition. Like the mythological gods, the archetypes are the formative principles, superordinate to human consciousness and will that structure, order, and animate our life experience. (158)

With further discussion, my sister priestess and I found we were on the same page after all and that our embodied feminist worldviews, while diverse and multifaceted, were interrelated and complimentary.

Sadly, in *Weaving the Visions: New Patterns in Feminist Spirituality*, Naomi Goldenberg argues that there is a schism between embodied spirituality and ecofeminist agency. She states, "Whether they are called Platonic forms, Jungian archetypes, or religious deities, theories based on their existence have colluded with devaluation of physical life and of the physical environment" (254). Yet for me, archetypes are entirely sacred; they are the wholeness of creation expressing itself. Furthermore, if they are life itself—and I believe all of life to be sacred—how could they be anything but absolutely divine?

Conclusion

Starhawk suggests that a psychology of liberation "can lead us to encounter the mysteries and must be rooted in an earth-based spirituality that knows the sacred as immanent" (21). For me, magic and mystery are inherent in my curious footsteps, my grateful heartbeat, and the smiles and tears of strangers. I can no longer fathom life without spiritual depth and breadth, even in the midst of suffering. Rick Tarnas speaks to the essence of my relationship with Nature when he says:

> When the primal person [and rather than "pre-industrial" I want to suggest a post-industrial stance, something akin to the "becoming indigenous" movement] walks out into the forest, or goes to the seashore, he or she experiences spirits in the trees and psychological and spiritual presences in nature. There is meaning in the movements of the wind and of the water currents. There are gods in the heavens. There are spirits in the forests and there is meaning that is conveyed by the movements of birds and animals and the weather, the rains and storms and wind. There are meanings in the cycles of the sun and the moon, in the conjunctions of the planets . . . . Nature is capable of holding meaning and communicating it to human beings. (Tarnas)

These Gaian cycles and movements form the core of my practice. Grateful for the elements, as my life force depends upon them, I honor the ecopsychological tenet that we are interdependent with them. My cosmological framework may never be a fixed entity, but I am sure that it floats around a core of embodied and practiced gratitude. I check its structural integrity regularly, inviting new embodied insights. I hope for a strong container—and a substantial amount of elasticity and curiosity—while I seek re-enchantment and dedication from the *inside out.*

CHAPTER 12

EXPLORING THE GOD/DESS— IMAGE WITHIN

Laurie Larsen

Without the intercession of the divine feminine we will remain in this physical and spiritual wasteland we have created, passing on to our children a diseased and desecrated world. (Llewellyn Vaughan Lee 4)

When I was a child, I had an innate sense of the sacred in all nature: sunlight filtering through the leaves of a mulberry tree caressing my closed eyelids and cheeks; sitting beside a rushing river bounding over glacier-strewn boulders, feeling a fine cool mist on my skin; the rich tangy smell of a warm pine forest; silently watching deer nibbling tall grasses in a sun-filled meadow; silky fur on my dog's head, his bright brown eyes looking into mine, mirroring our mutual love and devotion; expressing my praise to Artemis as wild, inspired movement while the heat-filled wind whips my old blue silk velvet goddess gown around my young body; gliding through cool water, sure that I sport a mermaid's tail. All these are memories of moments where I experienced harmony, grace, and divine immanence. These treasures are held in my heart's eye, whose calling up bestows peace. Add to this the myths and fairytales that my grandmother read to me, which also created a state of wonder and left me feeling woven into the great mystery of life. To this day, I read these ancient tales voraciously, always reveling in the ancient, powerful feminine.

As I moved towards adolescence, I became aware that the feminine aspect of the divine was sorely missing in the Presbyterian, Christian tradition in which I was being raised. In fact, I noticed that most histories, philosophies, and even the daily news, reflected a masculine world of achievements and ideas, values and rules of engagement. It was as if the feminine half of life was cloaked in invisibility. I saw that females did not hold a sacred place in Christianity. Even the first woman, Eve, was the seducer of Adam, and the cause of the fall from grace. Cursed by God Himself for her disobedience, Eve, and all women who followed, were condemned to be subservient helpmates and suffer terrible pain in childbirth forever more. I was around ten or eleven years old when it dawned on me—this means me!

A question began to press on me: Why were Greek myths considered just stories but the Bible stories were historical facts? Something didn't add up. Spurred on by the realization that Greek mythology represented an ancient culture's religion and that Greek and Christian myths shared storylines that seemed similar, I asked my minster to explain the difference. All he could offer me was, "There are some things you just need to have faith in."

Christianity ceased to resonate within me. I couldn't reverberate with the view that women and children were the chattel of men, or with the Old Testament stories portraying God as a vengeful, wrath-filled, irrational deity with too much power. His evolution into the all-good father who sacrificed his only son to pay for our sins was unthinkable, in any way that it was spun. I entered a long and lonely period of feeling bereft of any meaningful connection to the Divine.

Re-Discovering the Divine Feminine

In my thirties, I reconnected to the sacred feminine through the birth of my children. During each nine months of gestation, I was in awe. My body instinctively knew exactly what to do to create an intricate human body without a single directive from my mighty ego or intellect. My sensations and cravings intensified to help me know what to ingest and what to avoid. Subtle changes began in my body's shape, then came a fluttering sensation in my womb, soon followed by growth and more and more pronounced movements—how amazing! My dreams and connection to my unborn child, even shortly before conception, shocked me into wakeful consciousness. A mystery was afoot. The sense of a presence entering and leaving my baby's developing body throughout both pregnancies was astounding.

Here was a direct experience of a vibrant, alive, juicy, personally present divine Feminine, all around me, holding me, enfolding me, enacting life's cycle through me. I was a vessel, filled with the sensations of a life growing within my body—what a miracle. The very mystery that had been present with me always, hitherto reflected in my experiences with animals, nature, and my soaring imagination fed by dreams, creative expression, dance, fairy tales, and myths, was now palpable. It warmed me, awoke my heart, and instilled in me the burning desire to be the very best, most conscious mother I could be, from that time forth.

This commitment has been the most rigorous, challenging task, spiritual or otherwise, that I can possibly imagine undertaking. It has been like living inside a giant rock tumbler every day, for years. My rough edges have been ground into a slurry of devotion: my unquenchable love for the immense souls sprouting in the bodies of my babies ever polishing my being; the mirror of relationship reflecting both my darkness and my light, bringing consciousness to my automatic reactions, my self-centered longings, and my habitual ways of relating; my patience, acceptance, and endurance being honed and humbled in so many ways. For me, the heart's realm of intertwined, interdependent relationship is the archetypal Feminine, in all her fierce, dark, bright, and loving aspects. This is where the most profound meaning in life resides for me.

The Sacred Feminine Re-emerges

My mother, Jane, was always a muse. In 1987, she invited me to a lecture at the New York Open Center by Alice O. Howell, author of *Jungian Symbolism in Astrology*. I had just moved back to the United

States from London and was living in Brooklyn, New York, where I knew only a handful of people. The transformation I described above was well underway. Alice Howell was the embodiment of the Venus of Willendorf, with a shock of tousled, white hair. She was a feisty crone. I could easily imagine her trudging across the heath, with her druidic, antler-topped staff in hand. She recounted goddess histories and told of the sites she visited often in Scotland, in particular, the sacred Isle of Iona. I was shocked to learn about goddess traditions being re-discovered, re-invigorated! Why hadn't I heard about this?

Two days later, my mother gave me Marion Woodman's book, *The Pregnant Virgin,* and I was on my sacred Feminine search, discovering a world full of rich scholarship, including historical facts on the persecution, extermination, and abuse of countless women in the name of protecting and promoting Christianity. I was boiling with anger, but alone, and was now the mother of a tiny new baby. Moving three times in the first two years of her life, from New York to Vermont to Colorado, meant I had no community of women friends, just the invisibility and isolation that often accompanies motherhood in our culture. So I read and read and read in the cracks of time permitted a new mother.

Eventually the fires of outrage cooled, replaced by insights that many Jungian-inspired authors brought forth for me. Marion Woodman, Esther Harding, Robert Johnson, C. G. Jung, Laurens van der Post, China Galland, Marija Gimbutas, Joseph Campbell, Elinor Gadon, and Michele Cassou all taught me to see, to remember the long history of women-centered spirituality, to mark the re-emergence of the sacred Feminine, and to find images, thoughts, and words that for so many years lay underground, pushed into the darkest recesses of my body.

The breaking open of my heart through the process of birthing and mothering my daughter and then, three and a half years later, my son, brought all this to light. My deepest gratitude and enduring love go to my children who somehow, in some mysterious way, chose to entrust me as their mother. The vessel of my relationships has tempered and sustained me, challenged and nourished me deeply: my insightful, passionate daughter, Jessie, always a powerful feminine force showing me the yang fire assertion of the divine Feminine; my beautiful, wise son, Seann, from the beginning demonstrating the persuasive essence of the awakened heart of the divine Masculine; my courageous, tender daughter Manuela, who joined our family after a roundabout journey beginning in another loving family in Columbia, who shares the bold spirit of the sacred Feminine; and my husband Tom, who remained tenaciously engaged throughout heated battles with my emerging, fierce, feminine self, honoring and supporting the authority of my motherhood, while fashioning his own beautiful model of fatherhood.

If we are to survive this century, this age, this catastrophic mess we humans have created, it will be through joining the sacred Feminine and the sacred Masculine archetypal energies, remembering and inventing anew the celebration of sacred union that treasures, honors, and reveres all of nature.

PART III

EASTERN AND CONTEMPLATIVE SPIRITUALITY

CHAPTER 13

DISCOVERING THE BLISS OF THE GOD WITHIN

Jacqueline Fry

The depth psychology of C. G. Jung has helped me realize my own image of God. I was raised in a Christian church and taught to believe that God sat in the heavens and overlooked all of humanity. This God was a white-haired, crusty old fellow who controlled every part of our being, resembling Santa Claus, but on a much grander scale. Edward Edinger refers to an ancient author who commented on the tendency to anthropomorphize our conceptions of divinity: "If horses had a conception of God, it would be in the form of a horse, because that would be the only way they could conceive of it (25). He further elaborates on the epistemological implications:

> Indeed, it is how the Book of Job and the whole Old Testament describe Yahweh, as if he were a man—because there is no other way to describe him other than mythologically. According to Jung's epistemology, one cannot speak in any other terms except those categories and forms of perception and representation that are an innate part of our understanding process. The nature of the anthropomorphic God-image, that we experience and that the unconscious presents us with, our scriptures and mythological formulations, all of which were born of the psyche, all reveal themselves only through anthropomorphic imagery. (25-26)

I believe that religions have tended to remove divinity from human experience by emphasizing the need for a relationship to an external deity instead of an identity with the divine. Moreover, that relationship specifies a particular image of the deity and excludes others. The story of God's presence in Christ, for example, is generally taught by the church to be a singular and unique event. His virgin birth is not seen as a mythic metaphor but rather as a miracle that is believed to be a literal truth (Campbell, *Inner Reaches* 33). The consequence of the deification of Jesus is that Christians are alienated from their own inherent divinity (Campbell, *Bliss* 41). Joseph Campbell's approach to mythology provides an alternative way of understanding religious stories by revealing their powerful symbolic meaning—messages that speak directly to the heart. Mythic images, he explains, point beyond themselves and are "transparent to transcendence" (*Hero's Journey* 166). The hero's journey, in his view, represents the struggle of the individual to overcome the myriad obstacles of ordinary life and culminates in the recognition of the divinity within. As Campbell puts its, "The function of mythology is to connect you to your bliss and find where it truly is" (214).

When I meditate with a specific question in mind, knowing that wisdom is within reach, I discover the blissful nature of existence. Meditating in this way leads me deeper and deeper into a sea of great tranquility. Basking in the explosive sunlight of wisdom, I can absorb the experience of God. No intercessor is needed. I have found inner warmth and strength that I never dreamed possible. I experience an ocean of love and become aware of my true nature. Based on my practice of meditation, I have come to believe that a cosmic light shines within the nature of every individual. Once a person finds that light within, liberation from the ordinary travails of life is possible. When a person experiences this light, the divinity of the cosmos is also revealed. One must trust in the depths of the human soul to find one's way, placing one's trust in the great process of nature at work in the interior dimension of being. Faith in God can then blossom like a lotus flower. As this natural process unfolds, deep feelings of regard, love, and joy uplift one's life. When one has found the God within, he or she is ready to meet life to the fullest. This, in my view, is the fulfillment of the hero's journey, a path that can be discovered when one's God-image shifts from dependence on a transcendent Other to the divinity within the heart.

CHAPTER 14

BELIEVING IN THE SECULAR, KNOWING THE SACRED

Robert W. Guyker, Jr.

Grappling with the Divine is fraught with frustration. However, it can also be a source of jubilation. Standing at the apex of a young man's early inklings of God, and simply enjoying the imaginative process, I can say with some degree of comfort that I have yet to arrive at a concrete image of God. This, in part, is because I have accepted the limits of certainty and take seriously the art of joy. As Mark C. Taylor states, "The work of art is not only the created product but, more importantly, the *creative process* through which *any determinate form emerges*" (125). His last few words are essential to appreciating how the divine need not be restricted by categories nor by negation, but rather understood as an emergent impulse, best described as *autopoiesis* or self-creation.

One basic difficulty in any discussion of the divine is whether it is transcendent or immanent. If we reduce the divine to a single all-encompassing personage, that is, God, then is God here to intervene or as a *deus otiosus*, an idle god that, weary of us, has retired from the world and is no longer involved in its processes? Does the divine hide or reveal itself? If the divine truly is transcendent, let him or her do as she likes. If he or she is truly immanent, then let us revel!

I must be candid when I say that God was not a priority in my mind in my youth, but I do know that the existential experience dissolved once I deeply considered the idea of God. The mystery that allured me was uninhibited creative energy. I love to draw and at least through images I can play with serious things; otherwise, it is a grim affair. Because of my natural bent towards aesthetics—beauty, horror, form, and color—I enjoy studying and reveling in the colors of God. From an early age, I saw the divine in the imagination. Maybe this is why I loved mythology more than orthodox traditional pathways to God. By imagination I mean the living imaginal realm that any of us can feel operating when we are moved by our own epiphanies or when we snuggle up with a poem, book, painting or film and bask in the marvel of another's creative representation.

I once turned away from this imaginative impulse because I wanted to feel the presence of the divine. I prayed, meditated, and contemplated. In my undergraduate days in Virginia, I commuted on weekends to Maryland to spend the weekends with my parents, during those rough moments of life when I was experiencing growing pains, when trust felt defiled. Sometimes suffering enters our life to indirectly present what we thought we were seeking. External pain sent me inwards, where I found the divine. This experience of the divine was far beyond what I could imagine, not because it was awesome, sublime or beautiful; instead, it was no-thing or emptiness, experienced as an abiding presence. Once I got a taste of that emptiness, everything changed. A space was created inside. It's not a vacant hole, but a necessary pause in the stream of images and thoughts I found spinning in my mind.

I don't know if I ever found God, but I found the warmth of silence and that abiding emptiness. Whether life emerges out of it and resolves back into it, I don't know. Nevertheless, it has a presence and occupies a space within me. As Mark C. Taylor observes, "Since creativity is grounded in the groundless abyss of nothing, its expression is always new" (126).

In my doctoral studies, I have had the opportunity to inquire, in dialogue with my student colleagues, into the nature of myth, and discovered that the silence is not just in me, but in others, too. It's almost like a little ghost such that if you see it in another person it will notice you, hold its finger to its lips, say shush and wink. It is not my job to convince or convert anyone to the reality of it. We each arrive in our own way.

The ego dissolves when silence ends the oscillation between monologues and dialogues. Put in other words, soul revels in its own insights via inner speech (logos), and souls revel in hearing their narration (mythos) of those insights. Staying creative allows for the emergence of a third presence. We are no longer talking to ourselves or to some imaginary thing; we are listening in on the divine talking to itself. We may call it *autopoeisis*, *sui generis*, or *zi-ran* (of-itself-so). We can call it what we like, but we must recognize that the stories we tell shape our worldview and our images of the divine. We get the God or gods we deserve.

CHAPTER 15

DÀ TÓNG—THE GREAT HARMONY: WORLD, GOD-IMAGE, AND THE HUMAN SOUL

James Heaton

From the time of our beginning as homo sapiens, we have been religious animals. There is something in us that makes us stand in awe of the phenomena around us. The rising sun, a brilliant full moon, a violent thunderstorm, or the call of an owl in the lonely hours of the night—all bring something deep within us to the surface for a few, brief seconds. For a short time we stand arrested, in a state of wonderment. This is the beginning of both religion and science. The two are not mutually exclusive. Like most other aspects of the human milieu, they interact and cross-pollinate. Within the sciences, the religious impulse gives rise to curiosity and the desire for further discovery. Our inquisitive, knowledge seeking nature, applied to the realm of religion, gives us our pantheons and theologies, as well as our religious movements for justice and fairness. And all because of something deep that wakens and moves for a few all too brief seconds, in moments of cosmic beauty or sublimity. We call it a God-complex, a complex being a constellation of feelings and ideas surrounding a "nuclear element, a vehicle of meaning which is beyond the realm of conscious will" (Jacobi 8). This central element of the complex is numinous— there is no getting at what it is in itself (the Kantian *ding an sich*). This complex cannot be killed, nor can it be excised like some sort of cancer or damaged organ. Nor would we want it destroyed or disabled, for, once gone, we would feel its passing. Like the emptiness of lost love, we would feel a hole, an aching empty space where something important had once been. And in the end, it may well be our ability to love that we have lost.

Views of the God Complex

If we cannot know what a complex is at its center, we can know the emotions and symbols on the periphery of its existence. These are the feelings and images that arise during those epiphanies sparked by the world's beauty and sublimity. There are three approaches to these epiphenomena of the soul: what, to simplify, I call the secular, the psychological, and the spiritual.

Robert Heinlein, one of my favorite literary philosophers, once said, much to my chagrin, "The difference between science and the fuzzy subjects is that science requires reasoning, while those other subjects merely require scholarship" (Heinlein 366). This is the modernist, secular approach, with its scientific pronouncements and theoretical pontifications. Heinlein never really believed this for a moment or he would not have been writing "fuzzy fiction" (his own term). Nor would he have written what I consider one of the most beautiful expositions of the emotion of love that I have read: "Love is the condition in which the happiness of another person is essential to your own." I find fault with this view, as well, or I would have chosen some other path than that of a mythologist. Mark C. Taylor, in his work *After God*, found his own way through the perilous forest. There may, in fact, be no personal God to save us when things get tough. There may be no Being to remold our "sinful lives." There is, however, an intelligence behind the cosmos: call it Nirguna Brahman, or Shunyata, or Buddha Mind, or Dao, or Quantum Chaotic Inflation. It is the Ground of Being. This is the other half of the cosmos, the hidden half. The half that can be represented mathematically may be the half that we choose to see. It is not, however, the entirety of the system. Every yang has its yin.

Then there are the psychologists and their apologists. As a rule, their views are more in line with the secularists than with any of the theistic models. Consider Freud's views on the topic: religion and God are, at best, a baseless clinging to infantile behaviors and attitudes. Or consider the more current reduction of human interiority to the firing of neurons by neuropsychology. In contrast, the Jungian/archetypal approach to both psychology and religion has always taken a more compassionate and open-ended view. As Jung, in his essay "The Practical Use of Dream Analysis" notes, in relation to symbolism and the psyche:

> There are a great many of them [symbols], and all are individually marked by subtle shifts of meaning. It is only through comparative studies in mythology, folklore, religion and philology that we can evaluate their nature scientifically. (*CW* 16, para. 294-352)

Edward Edinger, in *The New God-Image*, goes one step further than his mentor in stating the nature of the God-complex. He makes a very clear and concise case for the fact that the whole religious phenomenon has its origin in ". . . realities which are derived from an inner, purposive, non-ego origin" (21). Religion and the religious impulse have their roots in the transpersonal realm of the collective unconscious.

According to both Jung and Edinger, this God-image is constantly evolving in response to human needs. As such, our image of God/ Ultimate Reality is, in many ways, radically different from the old one held by a medieval monk or peasant. It is exactly this evolutionary aspect of the transpersonal unconscious that enables religions and religious symbols to survive and remain relevant through massive changes in our philosophic and scientific paradigms.

The view that I label as spiritual would have little or no problem with either of these views. It would, however, add elements that are missing in a worldview based almost exclusively in the scientific method. These human elements—love, compassion, tolerance and humility—are qualities, not quantitative entities. They cannot be mathematically manipulated in the same ways in which we manipulate scientific data. There is, contrary to the speculations of some ethicists, no moral or humanitarian calculus with which to rate the impact of our actions or the correctness of our beliefs. There is only the correlation of our moral compass (our personal sense of goodness and truth) with the consequences of our actions for ourselves and for those around us.

His Holiness the Dalai Lama has no objection to science or the scientific method. In fact, he carries this approach to its reasonable conclusion. His answer to the phenomenon of religious experience is one of true pluralism. There are many religions because there are many different types of people and many different historical perspectives. No one path is any more inherently right than any other. This approach, of course, requires becoming familiar with the ideas of the "other." This line of reasoning states that, regardless of the sometimes radically different nature of belief systems, personal prejudices need to be put aside in favor of a compassionate understanding of the good done by all faith traditions.

I'm reminded of my first experience of China. I was culture shocked, and my jet lag was in full swing. Anyone who says that it is easy to be a minority in a foreign country is either very experienced (and more than a little jaded), or simply daft and not to be taken seriously. I was an outsider. Not only did I not speak or read Chinese languages with any degree of proficiency, I literally towered over most of the locals to the point that I became extremely self-conscious. I was *da laowai*—the big foreigner. My fight or flight response was so engaged that I could feel the moving air and vibration from incoming subway trains. This condition held for the first three of four weeks. Toward the end of this episode, however, I realized that, thanks to my panicked, cornered animal attitude, I was learning absolutely nothing from my new environment. With this realization, and a new and somewhat unwanted understanding of my uniqueness, I began to adapt.

The God/dess: My Personal, Evolving, God Image

Having been taught Christianity by my Episcopalian mother, it would have been easy for me to have simply followed in the rut worn by family and community. My father, a very open agnostic, had other ideas. His contribution was that I received an early and substantial education in both the hard and social sciences and the humanities. Being somewhere in between my mother's religious approach and my father's rationalism, I was raised in a sort of dynamic tension between religion and science. Much to the chagrin of both family and community, I developed more questions than they could answer. Even during my older childhood, I read voraciously in the sciences, mythology, archeology and anthropology. It wasn't until high school that I discovered neopaganism and, more specifically, the Hermetic tradition.

As it is said, the journey of a thousand miles begins with the first step. There had always been a certain degree of frustration with both the questions and the answers on both sides of the God debate. Neither absolute seemed absolutely true. My ambivalence persisted throughout my two-year stay in China. It was at this point that I realized that I was simply unaware of how to ask the right questions. And the *how* was all of it—I was asking the questions from the ivory tower of my intellect, while neglecting the real world needs of that intellect. What that intellect most needed was to be embodied, to be present here and now in the world. I thank my Chinese family for that realization. I have lost count of the times they told me that I "think too much and live too little."

What was it I wanted? I wanted a perspective balanced between the rational and the mythic, the Apollonian and the Dionysian. I wanted to be able to not only analyze the myths I was exposed to, but to feel them, to experience what it meant to live a mythology. It was the Chinese, who live according to a very similar ideal of balance and harmony, who showed me how to look. They didn't show me where to look; they simply pointed, suggestively, to the moon.

This is my God-image: balance, harmony of opposites, and comfort with paradox. In some ways, it is very much like all of the aforementioned meta-theories. I don't shy away from the sciences; there is absolutely no reason to do so. I have discovered a whole new set of interpretative tools in the Jungian/archetypal branch of psychology. My worldview has become much more pluralistic during my doctoral studies. There is, however, one element I was required to learn on my own, and learned because of the kindness and patience of my Chinese family. I have come to call this element mythic thinking: the ability to step out of the rationalistic Western mindset, and to actually feel the symbiosis of symbol and physical/psychological phenomenon that is a myth. This, for me, is the beginning of the study of myth—the origin of the Great Harmony (Dà Tóng) of my Chinese family, and that peace, within my mother's faith tradition, which passes all understanding.

CHAPTER 16

GOD WITHOUT AND WITHIN

By Gabriel Hilmar

I came to my notion of God through a circuitous path, much like the gnarled oak or the rambling willow. The way to God is often filled with pain and joy and then the realization of having been living God all along. God is love and love moves life:

> If you would kneel, kneel for love and beauty,
> For the joy that is yours every waking moment,
> For the love that humbles,
> For the individual, sentimental journey through life.

Love, much like God, is a difficult and highly subjective term to define. Yet we all know in the marrow of our bones when we are experiencing love and when we feel alienated from it. Love flows through our lives and humbles us before its vastness. The universe, nature, and our own selves are manifestations of this love.

Taoism doesn't differentiate or create a hierarchy around the source of all things or its manifestations. The Tao is inclusive and embraces both as one. This inclusivity is quite different from the Western religions of revelation (Judaism, Christianity, and Islam) that desacralize nature, though the mystical traditions of Kabbalah, Gnosticism, and Sufism are an exception to this and are rooted in both nature and time, enabling practitioners to experience timelessness through living mindfully in the present moment.

There are many mysteries that our conscious concept of love or God cannot embrace. What happens with loss and death? Nature gives life but it also takes it away. Perhaps one's vision of God would be different if stranded in the middle of the ocean than it would be for a suburban bourgeois in an SUV, sheltered from discomfort. For one, God would seem vast, frightening, monstrous, and awe-inspiring, and for the other, friendly, sleepy and forever cradling. Yet, don't both experience death and aging? No one is free from this inevitability, not even the wealthy. If we are open and honest, allowing ourselves to sink a little into the dark depths of human suffering, we see God's shadow:

> God is love and love a wound.
> Poor bastards you wound with the grief stricken harpoon,
> jabbed through your own flesh,
> carrying tombstones with your own names inscribed.
> Retreating into avarice and insanity
> the black hole lurks in every one of us.
> Crowded aloneness chokes the spirit
> and annihilates hope in a mechanized waste.

Despair is natural in the face of unbridled suffering, whether in the stranded lonely soul amidst the ocean or the Prozac dependent suburban driver drowning in exhaust. It is ordinary, simple, everyday beauty that has the power to pull us out of hell. Victor Frankel realized this in his beloved flowers growing in the cracks of Auschwitz concrete. Here is my ode to Frankel:

> Outside I saw a small flower,
> nothing more than a child's wink.
> It made me smile.
> I breathed a sharp breath and awoke
> once again to the magic.
> That one little moment brought the sun.

Even in the darkest parts of existence, some form of love shines through. Often God's love goes unnoticed. If God's love only came in the form of Dante's siren call of ethereal, beatific bliss, then we would not receive the small, seemingly insignificant earthly gift of a flower or the smile of a loved one. The small is indeed great. Why else would Buddha have held up a flower as his sermon? These small, sentimental, personal details make up a life with all its nostalgia and memories. We live and experience life as individuals, therefore, our own unique path has its own story:

> Into the kingdom that was always there I have entered. Beatrice
>   so heavenly,
> I choose earthly Venus, flower of the one tree, for my soul.

In our heavily mechanized world, God becomes important as a symbol of nature and as such, a kind of return to our own nature as animals of the planet. God in this sense stands in opposition to the insane notion of eternal economic expansion at the cost of our own humanity and the earth as a whole. I feel we must return to this sense of God as nature if we are to survive. No longer can a dissociated concept of God divorced from nature be a tenable, sustainable image. We must invest in the planet and revitalize our connection with the animistic energies of nature that are right inside of us, seen most readily in children's play and active imagination.

In *After God*, Mark C. Taylor stresses the urgency of the global problems that confront us all. He writes, "A sense of crisis pervades the world today. As old figures and patterns break down, people realize that we are at a tipping point, but they cannot yet discern the contours of the so-called new world order" (348). He continues to discuss this tipping point that cannot yet be fully understood in the new world order and is not merely causing typical generational anxiety, but rather, is shocking the new generation with an unprecedented rate of change. Many social customs and institutions that once held value for decades or even centuries are being discarded as outdated or obsolete. There is no longer an opportunity to come to know local organizations and communities on a deeper, more personal level. Life has become corporatized, leaving us to live impersonal, anonymous lives; individuals are faceless worker-slaves and their very life force is used as energy to power the machine. Because of this alienation from nature, both outer and inner, many find themselves drawn to a simpler way of being when material possessions cease to fill the gaping hole of unfulfilled existence.

In Western religious thought, humans become like gods over nature and cease to wonder in awe at nature's vastness. Only in extreme circumstances, like natural disasters, do people wake up to nature's wonder through an apocalyptic disaster. How do we cure this sickness of being orphaned from our own planet? The God-image in a society affects people's behaviors and attitudes. If a society has a violent God, it is apt to be violent; if it has a God who crushes nature, destruction will follow.

What, then, does sentimentality have to do with the awesome power of God? Consider the image of Buddha giving a silent sermon by holding up a flower. In the West we have the image of the sacred heart of Jesus, a human embodiment of divinity who suffers alongside us. Perhaps these old gods can blend in with the new gods and a new world order can emerge, in which we feel the planet to be living deity. Through attention and mindfulness, to little seemingly insignificant things, like flowers and the smile of a loved one, we can reclaim our place here that belongs in the now. As William Blake proclaims:

> Hear the voice of the bard [the God within us],
> Who present, past and future, sees . . . .
> Turn away no more;
> Why wilt thou turn away?
> The starry floor,
> The watery shore,
> Is given thee till the break of day. (18)

C. G. Jung speaks of the importance of living a life with meaning. Joseph Campbell states that life has no inherent meaning, only the experience of being alive. Perhaps both are true. We seek meaning as a way of delving deeper into life's wonder and mystery, which we can use as a tool when grace and inspiration hide or falter. But we must also experience life in its unfolding moment, without seeking, which comes to us like a lover in the night. Knowing when to open to these moments is as important as seeking meaningful structure in one's life. These moments can often come through poetry and music. As a Flamenco song expresses it, "Your love seems like a bunch of grapes; the freshness comes first, the drunkenness after" (Pohren 119). This drunkenness is fiercely individual; it includes a divine drunkenness that is inspired by the mysterious muse that we know not, yet see if our eyes are open. When we open up to the wonder of the universe, then we are walking the sacred path of love:

> My heart has chosen the path with heart.
> The rustling trees, the shimmering moonlight,
> the quaking heart that loves openly,
> yet at times sentimentally just for the one, the little, the dear.
> I choose earthly Venus,
> I choose the pain,
> I choose the old friend,
> the flash of light that is a lifetime.
> I choose the Bard's poetic present.

CHAPTER 17

THE FACE OF GOD:
MUSINGS OF A NEW MOTHER

Rachel Shakti Redding

Before I gave birth to my child, my child did not yet exist. I could not miss one who did not exist. Therefore, I did not understand when my friends, who were already parents, expressed their concern, suggesting that I might miss something important by not having a child. "What is the value of having a child?" I ruminated. Devoting resources to one human being seemed inefficient when there are so many children already among us, vying for our time, food, and love. Now that my daughter has arrived, I look into her eyes, vibrant with the light of vitality, and realize her intrinsic worth. She is of value, it seems, simply because she exists. Perhaps the purpose of life, then, is life itself.

Such are the musings of a new mother. There is arguably nothing more worthy of contemplation than the birth of a child except, reasonably, the death of a loved one or friend. As I relish the newness of my baby Marley's tiny life, I witness my mother in a state of terminal illness. My mother is in a constant cycle of dying and being born again as she revisits the crooks and valleys of her life path, examining her decisions along the way. Feeling gratitude for her experiences, she is, at the same time, deeply sorrowful. She is preparing to leave her body, her world, and everything she has ever known. She dreams of heaven and treasures the ideals inspired by her Midwestern Dutch upbringing within the Christian Reformed Church. Through this faith, she finds peace.

As a child, my mother shared with me her faith and, with it, the values of compassion, love, and forgiveness. To her, Jesus is God and God is love. Love, for her, is the highest truth. Now, in turn, I am a mother. It is my turn to share visions, hopes, and ideas with my own daughter. Traveling farther than my mother ever did, I witness worldviews far beyond my own. Each person I meet has something valuable to share and the more I understand, the less I know. What do I want to teach my child about God?

My mother- and father-in-law vie for the baptism of my daughter's little head. They pray for her soul's salvation through the power of the Catholic Church. My teacher, a native of South India, offers the blessings of the Goddess instead. She chants mantras that invoke the Divine Mother's protection. At her birth, however, it was the Krishna mahamantra that heralded Marley's entrance into the world. Her godmother, a modern day *gopi*, sang "Hare Krishna, Hare Krishna, Krishna Krishna, Hare Hare." With that simple phrase, she dedicated my new baby's soul to Krishna. Marley will learn about animal totems and nature spirits from her godfather; he calls upon the Great Spirit for her protection and her prosperity.

Our home is filled with gilded deities. On occasion they become fully animated as I adorn them with gifts and songs. Most often, however, they serve as symbolic, dynamic, psychological reminders—relics of my intentions and aspirations. Marley dances to kirtan music performed by Krishna Das. Her eyes light up with recognition as he sings, "Oh Hanuman, where did you get that ring?" This catchy tune is a modern day hymn of the mythic Hindu epic, the *Ramayana,* with its reverence for Rama and his devotional monkey-god friend. Our life is a smattering of religious perspectives and spiritual tributes. I particularly appreciate the openness of the Hindu traditions and their acceptance of the multiplicity of religious experience. In *Toward a True Kinship of Faiths*, the Dalai Lama honors Hinduism's lack of dogmatism by observing that "the various religions are different languages through which God speaks to the human heart" (49). The greatest secret of India may be that God is revealed in every person (51). For the Hindu, God is certainly not dead. The fire of God cannot and will never burn out, as long as there are sentient beings to spark the flame. When referring to Hindu dharma, the Dalai Lama highlights the importance of contemplative awareness. "The quest for truth," he writes, "lies within the heart of human life" (44). Experiential knowledge of the Self is realization of the God within, which Hindus refer to as *atman* (46).

In the *Bhagavad Gita*, Krishna encourages Arjuna to follow his true dharma or life path: "It is better to perform one's own duties imperfectly than to master the duties of another" (Easwaran 94). In the words of Jung, I wish for Marley to "follow [her] libido wherever it takes [her]" (qtd in Edinger 17), so that she will become a genuinely individuated and whole person as she learns from her mistakes. I deeply desire my child to have her own experience of God, to choose the path, the face, and the name of God that resonates with her authentic heart. Discovering her own expression, unique from all others, is the only way for her to truly know God in the manner that Jung proclaims, "I don't have to believe, I know" (qtd in Edinger 30). With this knowledge, she can savor an intimate wisdom within the subjectivity of her psychological awareness and realize the value of all others' perspectives. She can distinguish her ego from her deeper Self and therefore be moved by religious realities arising from her inner psyche (Edinger 21). She can know her Self as limitless *atman*, one with the source of love.

As much as I can subscribe to the Kantian notion of subjectivity—that there are limitations on what can be known—I am compelled to follow a thread of possibility. The thread originates outside of the psyche as a sovereign entity and independent of the psyche. The divine fiber then weaves its way into the mind of humanity. Here it grows within both our conscious and unconscious minds as a direct reflection and fragmentary perception of the highest truth. Perhaps, akin to Plato's ideal, because of its existence, we can begin to know it. What is known is a light that exists with or without the awareness of sentient beings. May Marley look at the sky and know that others, across the globe, are looking at the same sky too. By and by, we all see the color blue.

I am not attached to the notion of Brahman, the Hindu name for the supreme, ubiquitous reality. The mythology of this preeminent and autonomous being may take the shape of the Christian father God, the pure consciousness of Shiva, or the creative power of a goddess. It is this transcendent God-image, however, which inspires me to beauty and that moves me to love. For Jung, the real object of one's religious affection is a pre-existing archetypal pattern in the human psyche. Yet even Jung's explanation seeks to harness that which cannot be contained, and I am not wholly convinced. It is the question itself that drives me, not the answer. In the stillness of meditative contemplation, both the questions and answers become superfluous. Here, in what the Upanishads called the "lotus of the heart," experiential knowledge feels nothing like religion; it simply feels like love. Of course, that experience comes from my subjective awareness and my subjective awareness is what I have to offer Marley. My own interpretation is all that I can give.

May I offer my daughter an example of how to embody creativity, personal power, and joy so that these qualities will, in turn, blossom within her being. May she be peace seeking and inspired by life. May she engage in everyday rituals that infuse her life with meaning and a direct experience of the sacred. May she possess passion for beauty as well as compassion for those experiencing sorrow. May the quest for truth be an abiding aspiration so that she may experience *moksha* or spiritual freedom, which Hindus regard to be the ultimate purpose of a human birth (Dalai Lama 45). May my little one, ultimately, embrace and be embraced by love. Love is, for me, the highest truth. I am not so different, really, from my mother.

In my baby's eyes, I see the face of God; in her existence, I am more truly and deeply aware of what God means to me. She is, for me, a mirror to my own soul. Could the sole purpose of life be simply for life's own sake? Perhaps this is what we human beings stand to offer one another: a life-affirming reminder of our highest nature—our divinity. If so, then every new child carries that spark of recognition; each of my relations abides in the house of truth; and every face is indeed the face of God.

PART IV

ATHEIST AND SECULAR SPIRITUALITY

CHAPTER 18

MAKING A STAND

Timothy Hall

Mark C. Taylor's *After God* is a remarkable work. At first, as a person immersed in academia, I felt overwhelmed and humbled by his stature as a scholar. The intricate strands of logic that he weaves together, each one filled with meticulous research into the history and development of Western consciousness, are masterful in the way that symphonies are masterful. As I let the full weight of this very heavy book affect my way of being in the world, I realized that I would never be able to accomplish the same type of work, at least not in that realm. For a few weeks, I occasionally thought about that and a part of me mourned. The thought would come to me that, if I had made different choices when I was much younger and working on a BA in philosophy, I might have gotten to a place where I could have worked on a tome as complicated as the one that Taylor, after years of study, produced.

Eventually I remembered that I had made those choices, eons ago, for very good reasons. I had come to a place intellectually where I *knew* (in the way that I knew things then) that both the life and the consciousness of an individual were art forms. I did not want to do inauthentic art and to continue in philosophy in the USA at that time would have required me to do so. I turned down the chance of doing graduate work at McGill University in Canada, where there were living and breathing phenomenologists (in contrast to the raging proponents of linguistic analysis that reigned in America at that time). Instead, I started blowing glass. It was the right choice for me. Therefore, I do not mourn the things that I chose not to do. Nor do I criticize Mark

C. Taylor for not becoming a glassblower. As he proposes at the end of *After God*, I acknowledge and embrace the diversity of the choices that others have made.

Taylor highlights that diversity by exemplifying his notion of *figuring* through an extremely complex system of *schemas*, in which he analyzes the relationship of meanings provided by those constructions within a matrix of other meanings. He does this in a way that is reminiscent of a *maestro* directing a symphony. Because of this, to critique Taylor's squashing of Venn diagrams into ovals so that he can claim them as his own, or his purloining of Edmund Husserl's intentionality and C. G. Jung's archetypes within a blaze of re-defining and re-wording fireworks, seems petty. There may be some arrogance in *After God*, but it is well earned. It is a magnum opus. It is also, as I have believed human creations to be since I was that young man years ago, a work of art. It is such powerfully constructed art, so convincingly presented, that it is iconic. When the many impressions left by his work are considered, they leave one with the feeling that he has found a way of making sense out of the world.

As a work of art, another look at *After God* is warranted. Taylor, in a way that is (to use one of his terms) "isomorphic" to Jacques Derrida's concept of language as a distorted reflection, calls art a "disfigurement" of the near-infinite details of objective reality that are present to consciousness as subjective sensation and/or subjective intellectual perception.

Both Derrida's *deconstruction* and Taylor's *disfigurement* are dependent upon Husserl's concept of a transcendental ego that makes choices about which elements of the world of subjective consciousness require attention. Arguably, Derrida and Taylor both assume some vague or ambiguous form of Jung's archetypal structures as well. In any case, deconstruction and disfigurement are actions or choices made by the conscious mind; to a great extent, they are directed by the unconscious mind. This is Husserl's thinking and, respectively, Jung's.

Here is where the *after* in *After God* comes into play. After writing the text, Taylor's words were transformed into an object through a daunting process that involved pen-to-paper, paper-to-publisher, publisher-to-printer, and so on, until it reached an eventual reader. He projected his fractal-like crystalline structures into the co-evolving, co-emergent world (which includes cyberspace), where they were objectified. After that, they were re-integrated into the consciousnesses of other people. Like a trail of breadcrumbs in a strange forest, the various objective links can be followed from a book-in-hand back to the mind of Mark C. Taylor.

In a sense, this is incarnation: the subjective is turned into the objective. Peter L. Berger describes this process in *The Sacred Canopy: A Sociological Construction of Religion*, as the way in which understandings of the numinous are created and become culturally dominant. His looping structure of projected, objectified, amplified, and re-integrated subjective understanding is a very simple diagram of the groundwork of culture. It is also a description of the processes of artistry, and in this sense, Taylor's *After God* was the result of forces that are isomorphic to the complicated histories and intents that produce any item in the *made world* of human existence.

With that in mind, I realized that for me, the equivalent of that tome would have been a large and complicated glass vase. Both the book and the glass piece are created from a stance that implies a response to the numinous, as are the actions of any other individual, whether they involve planting crops, raising a family, holding a job, falling in love, or drinking a beer in the afternoon. When we face the unknown possibilities of the *mysterium tremendum*, the future, or the import of the past, we do so upon a platform of belief.

As Taylor observes, "the gods or their functional equivalents do not simply disappear but go underground, where they continue to support human life" (10). He does not clearly define what he means by "underground." The pantheon of gods in James Hillman's archetypal psychology, however, as the home of templates for understanding and behavior, is probably the functional equivalent of that unobserved place. Taylor's underground seems to be isomorphic to the unconscious mind, but filled with matrices and schema instead of gods and goddesses. In any case, Taylor felt the necessity to write books to represent his understanding of existence. I felt the necessity, for many years, to make vases and bowls in order to secure my psyche to the planet. The advantage of my stance is that no one argues with a vase.

CHAPTER 19

MARK C. TAYLOR'S *AFTER GOD:* CRITICAL REFLECTIONS

Daniel Ortiz

In *After God*, Mark C. Taylor has created a masterful analysis of religion. Applying complex adaptive system principles to religion, Taylor gives meticulous attention to the ways in which religion is intricately connected to the social, economic, political, and technological aspects of culture. The scope and depth of his analysis is far-reaching and illuminating, so much so that I was astonished by what is missing. Little attention is given to the insights available from depth psychology, especially the contributions by C. G. Jung and James Hillman. Taylor has produced a magnificent work, but despite its richness, speculation regarding the book's omissions is both necessary and fruitful.

In the first chapter entitled "Theorizing Religion," Taylor points out that "religion is not limited to what occurs in churches, synagogues, mosques, and temples; rather, there is a religious dimension to all culture" (3). He goes on to say that "religion, moreover, is often most influential where it is least obvious" (3). Those familiar with Mircea Eliade, who is cited by Taylor, are also likely to be familiar with the contributions of C. G. Jung. It would serve Taylor's academic purpose to enhance his description of religion by referencing Jung, to support his statement that the concept of religion is not limited to the sacred. Jung's extensive writings on religion and culture demonstrate the complexity of mythology embedded in the nature of society; however inconspicuous it may be, it is nevertheless formidable. Jung's ideas about the permeation of religion and myth in secular aspects of society mirror Taylor's assertions concerning religion.

By identifying religion as a complex adaptive system, Taylor recognizes the spontaneous, adaptable, and codependent phenomena within a system. He acknowledges the inherent entropy within a religious system and examines how the structures within that system interact and impact one another. Because religion is so steeped in human psychology, culture and mythology, one must wonder what new insights Taylor might offer by including Jungian and archetypal depth psychological approaches. The gravity of these perspectives bears significantly on matters regarding society, because these fields draw from empirical conclusions based on a wide range of historical and anthropological data that establish cultural similarities regardless of epoch or culture.

Taylor surgically deconstructs complex phenomena within religion. He describes the interrelated dynamics of religion and illustrates the same dynamic among differing religious traditions, thereby providing an insightful account of religious evolution. Taylor describes the synchronic and diachronic axes of religion, how schisms develop within a single religious tradition. He observes that "religious traditions and cultural institutions tend to be deeply resistant to change" and that there is "growing volatility and insecurity" within a religion in itself (23). Taylor is essentially describing a drive towards disequilibrium, a tipping-point or a "self-organized criticality" within religion. This concept may be uniquely contextualized and further elucidated by James Hillman's concept of *pathologizing*. In *Re-Visioning Psychology*, he explains that pathologizing is "the psyche's autonomous ability to create illness, morbidity, disorder, abnormality, and suffering in any aspect of its behavior and imagine life through this deformed and afflicted perspective" (57). The spontaneity in psychological pathologizing reflects the changes inherent in religious evolution. Such phenomena are not diseases or problems to be conquered. They are natural events to be identified with the original purpose of religion: to enrich or connect individuals and cultures to soul. As Hillman observes, "where there is a connection to soul, there is psychology;

where not, what is taking place is better called statistics, physical anthropology, cultural journalism or animal breeding" (xviii).

Religion, including the concept of God or the gods, is a system as much as it is a psychological event. Therefore, it is evident that religion, too, carries with it the psychology of humanity. When Taylor writes of the reaction to self-doubt within religion, he is referencing a psychological complex, a feeling-toned group of representations in the unconscious of the psyche. A religion has a psychology just as an individual does; both intermittently pathologize. Including theorists such as Jung and Hillman within Taylor's work would augment and amplify his otherwise insightful discussion of the pervasive influence of religion in contemporary culture.

As a reader, engaging Taylor's book evokes a complex within me— complex and contrary emotions—that serve as *prima materia* for my own scholarly work. On the one hand, I feel envious of Taylor's academic achievement. What a beautiful book! On the other hand, I am happy that I do not write in the manner Taylor does. His dense prose and extensive analysis neglect certain aspects of the psychological and existential struggles that are the stuff of daily life. This form of complexity is no less important than the historical trajectories and interrelated systems that are the focus of Taylor's attention. I am haunted by the spectral abstractions of academia and simultaneously enthralled by the romanticism of theory. With regard to the way in which I wrestle with the mystery of a God-image, I can only try to blend what I have conceptualized with what I feel. I am ultimately unsure what God is and I can only attempt to identify the moments and visions in which I am in the presence of the subtle animation put forth by God or a god. For me, God is love and God is death; it is mainly through these two critical life elements that I see any semblance of a God. Torn between multiple worlds, I am likely to continue my struggle to re-mythologize my ideas of God and Self, Eros and Thanatos, and all of the numinous things in-between.

CHAPTER 20

THE QUANTUM GOD

John Redmond

What if God had a cat named Schrödinger? And, in His or Her infinite kindness, decided to place this kitty in a sealed box with a capped bottle of hydrogen cyanide? In addition, the box is fitted with a Geiger counter containing small traces of a radioactive substance that within an hour will see at least one of the atoms decay. If the atom decays, the Geiger counter will discharge and pull a lever that removes the cap of the bottle, releasing the hydrogen cyanide inside the box. This scenario is a nearly eighty-year old "thought-question" posed by Erwin Schrödinger to describe the enigma of quantum mechanics. As long as God does not observe the contents of the box, the decaying atom will simultaneously exist in a state of superposition—both decayed and not decayed. Furthermore, as the cat is also made up of particles, it will simultaneously be both dead and alive until someone, like God, observes it. At which point one of the realities will collapse and the cat will either be dead or alive. The fact that in quantum mechanics the act of observing creates a reality is surely among the most puzzling and disturbing discoveries in the history of humanity. Quantum mechanics denies the existence of a physical reality independent of its conscious observation.

Quantum theory is one of the most successfully tested theories in existence. No known prediction has ever been found to be in error. It is the fundamental landscape on which all physics and reality reside. A third of our economy depends on products that utilize quantum mechanics, such as transistors, MRI's, and lasers. In the

1970s, quantum cosmologist John Wheeler drew a picture of an eye looking back toward the Big Bang and asked, "Does looking back 'now' give reality to what happened 'then'?" It has also been speculated that just postulating a theory that is not in conflict with any previous observation actually creates a new reality (Kuttner 205-206).

To take it a step further, by posing the question "Is there a God?" we are creating a situation where God exists in a superposition of both existence and non-existence. We may be, in fact, quite literally creating God, as nonsensical as that may seem. C. G. Jung asks, "Is the creator conscious of himself?" (Edinger 64). The true mystery of quantum mechanics is how consciousness and reality are related. If we are unsure of this most fundamental question, then the question "Is there a God?" seems superfluous.

The existence of a supreme deity, or some sort of intentional organizing process, is one of the deepest personal and philosophical questions we can ask ourselves. However, these questions must incorporate the most current scientific reality—even if that reality is a not quite what one would have hoped.

One solution to the quantum enigma is the many-worlds theory or Multiverse. In this scenario, God's cat is quite literally both alive and dead. He is alive in this reality, but dead in another reality or universe. That could also mean that God does not exist in this universe, but does exist in another. Imagine that at this very moment, there is "another me" giving this exact presentation to this exact audience. In another universe, things might be only slightly different, for example with me wearing a red shirt instead of a blue one. Obviously the theological and personal implications are profound in such a bizarre reality. This is an extreme example, but also one of the more popular models that the theoretical physicists and mathematicians are exploring.

In his book *Toward a True Kinship of Faiths,* the Dalai Lama opens with a chapter entitled "Leaving the Comfort Zone." It does not have to do with physics, but rather refers to his eye-opening engagement with other religious traditions that, in his youth, seemed inconsequential when compared to his Buddhist beliefs. "Looking back," he says, "I see that, my crucial learning experience was the shift that took place away from a parochial and exclusivist vision of my own faith as unquestionably the best" (17). This lesson can also be applied to the "opening up of one's mind," away from the security of the Biblical and Newtonian worldview and into a world that is infinitely exciting and just as infinitely disturbing. For it necessitates a "leaving of one's comfort zone," a walking into the forest where it is darkest and there is no way or path.

What is my idea of God? It is the ever-expanding cosmological worldview in which six hundred years ago, Copernicus viewed the edge of the universe as the edge of our solar system. A few centuries later, it was determined that the Milky Way, more than a billion times larger than our local solar system and one which takes over 100,000 years to traverse while moving at the speed of light, encapsulated our entire existence. Now the Milky Way is but one of billions of galaxies, each grander and more vast than the next. My idea of God is the vibrating particles mysteriously jumping into and out of existence at the quantum level, existing both here nor there. For me, God is connotative of the mystery that seems inexhaustible in its ability to provide sublime and awestruck wonder. For me, God is my two cats, Sachi and Penny, who never got into that darn cyanide box and are waiting for me to come home.

CHAPTER 21

IS GOD DEAD?

Haydeé Rovirosa

Despite the fabulous technological achievements that provide us with comfort and security in life that other ages could only dream of; despite the astounding discoveries of modern science that have revealed the fundamental secrets of the physical and biological universe; despite proliferating knowledge in the fields of history, anthropology, sociology, and psychology; and despite the constant stimuli intended to entertain and divert us from our anxieties—something (or someone) seems to be missing.

The death of God is one of the defining events of our time. It marks the end of one worldview, but opens the possibility of a new one. The proclamation of Friedrich Nietzsche captures our situation: "Whither is God? . . . I shall tell you. We have killed him—you and I. All of us are his murderers . . . . God is dead. And we have killed him" (23). The truth of the matter is that gods do die when they no longer speak to our experience of existence, our thirst for being, and our quest for meaning; when they become silent in the face of the deepest challenges of our lives; when their absence becomes more apparent than their presence; when the concept of God that we have been given no longer matches our experience of the world. When God becomes silent, it means we have lost a shared myth, a common "meaningful story" that can make sense of the world and our place in it.

The assertion of the death of God need not necessarily be a claim of atheism. For some, the death of God means not the loss of the

God-experience, but rather, the failure of a culturally transmitted image of God that no longer rings true. The Western experience of the death of God is, in fact, a profound deconstruction of God conceptualized as an anthropomorphic, monarchical, patriarchal, static, all-controlling, wholly Other. The silence of God may, for some, be the silence of absence and death, but for others it may be the silence of mystery and a new kind of presence. The death of God has not diminished the insatiable human longing for meaning.

The death of God is not only a phenomenon of the absence or denial of God. Beyond this, the death of God creates, to use Martin Heidegger's terminology, a clearing, an open space in which something new can emerge (29). The death of God is actually the necessary prerequisite for a more profound vision of God to emerge. We live in an age defined by the death of God, but a new spiritual worldview, a new mythic story is emerging around us. There is, I am convinced, a new experience of God or divinity arising to fill the open space left by the death of the "Other" God. I am also convinced that the encounter with this "new" God is being articulated within a variety of contemporary fields of thought such as mysticism, science, literature, psychology, ecology, feminism and art, among others. I argue that, although from very different perspectives and methods, the insights of the different fields mentioned define the outlines of a new mythos—a new *mythopoiesis* of God, a new meaningful story. This new vision of God implies a new vision of human wholeness and how we relate to each other and to the world.

The vision of God emerging in our time can best be described as a "poetics," rather than a theology or philosophy or science of God. "Poetics" is used here in the original Greek sense of the word *poiesis* meaning "to bring forth through creative making." Poetics—of which art is one manifestation—"is the process of bringing forth into presence, and giving symbolic expression to a vision that has, until apprehended and expressed, been hidden and silent" (Plato 26). Art, then, discloses that which has hitherto been concealed. This mode of experiencing truth has been central to the work of a number of contemporary artists. For them, a receptive and creative attentiveness to what reveals itself in experience is the authentic way of apprehending the deepest truths of existence.

The vocation of artists is to bring to consciousness and expression the full range of the human drama of existence in all its tragedy and glory, from the longing for wholeness and meaning to the height of the mystical encounter with the divine. Art, therefore, is not merely an aesthetic activity; it is, like philosophy and religion, a path and a way of being. Another remarkable characteristic of art is that the appreciation of an artwork is often determined by the attunement of the spectator. To illustrate this using a visual example, consider a leaf falling from a tree, such a common event that we rarely even notice it. And yet, in a Zen story, the full and true witnessing of one falling leaf may be precisely what brings enlightenment. In either case, it is simply a leaf falling. In the first instance, it is, as far as we can see, nothing more than that. In the moment of enlightenment, however, the falling leaf somehow becomes the mysterious catalyst that triggers the experience and remains ever after a symbol. Art can be like this.

When the one who experiences the falling leaf is in the proper attunement, it discloses a kind of reality not seen before. Such an experience of art demonstrates that the deeper we penetrate the mystery of existence, the more we realize that reason and logic alone are inadequate to convey the reality of that dimension of experience. In the realm of art we move from statements of fact to symbols, metaphors, and myths, inspired intuitively through the creative imagination. The smallest event can become an epiphany. This seeing is an encounter with the divine in both its mystery and its presence. Art, then, is a form of revelation of the divine, but, as with all true revelation, it is not the transmission of a body of propositional doctrines or theological conceptions. It discloses, rather, something of a mysterious reality that remains always mysterious no matter how much is disclosed. The prophetic task of art is to connect with the spectator in a way that speaks to, but does not construct a wall around, the reality described. Maintaining the dialectical dance of knowing and unknowing, saying and unsaying, keeps the clearing of wonder and mystery open for further revelation. This attunement protects the seeker from becoming trapped in mythologies that reify and literalize

God as Other, father, Supreme Being, or Higher Power. This opens up a space in which humankind can go about its deepest calling: to end suffering and cultivate joy in individuals, families, communities, ecosystems, and the planet as a whole.

The trauma of the death of God may be overcome through the rebirth of God in new images. "Heidegger has called the frightening and attracting space where God used to be the 'clearing' (*Lichtung*) which can best be inhabited in the mode of receptivity and non-imposition (*Gelassenheit*)" (Wennemyr 55). In order for a new image of God to emerge, we must be able to allow ourselves to experience the divine from within the potentially traumatic empty space that has opened in the wake of the death of God. Only through an alert and receptive awareness can a new vision of the mytho-poiesis of God emerge.

Many voices have been invoked that express a new mystical image of God in the postmodern age. As Edward Edinger observes, "We are right on the verge of witnessing the birth of a new God-image" (96). Mark C. Taylor titles his book *After God*, but how is *after* to be understood? Taylor provides the answer: "On the one hand, to come after is to be subsequent to what previously has been, and on the other hand, to be after is to be in pursuit of what lies ahead . . . . Far from simply destructive, disfiguring is the condition of the possibility of creative emergence" (345). In the words of Gregory of Nyssa: "Finding God consists in endlessly seeking God" (qtd in Panikkar 144). This is yet another paradox that helps us understand that contradictoriness is what life is all about.

CHAPTER 22

ON THE OTHER HAND:
AN ATHEIST REFLECTS ON GOD

Angela Sells

I'm touched by an angel when you
enter the room. You are a beautiful saint.
My heart's filled with love when I
see you, the power in me inside, the string from
your heart to mine
is the electricity that never dies.

I remember writing this poem after having a fantastic vision of God during a trip to the liminal, in-between world of anesthesia, when I had my gallbladder removed at age seven. I remember how strongly I felt about my God-image—my Beloved—which I envisioned as a big ball of golden light, providing warmth, love, and safety. I remember this and I miss it.

I lost my God-image that next year after reading *The Diary of Anne Frank* and learning about how she died in the Holocaust. For a little while, I was obsessed with the notion of converting to Judaism, out of some notion of solidarity, but in truth, I had lost my religion completely. I think I have spent my entire life trying to reconcile religion and these darker realities of humanity. Even now I am writing my dissertation on the diaries of a young Jewish woman who died in the Holocaust.

I should make the distinction between personal religion and organized religion (or organized belief), because my opinion on the two is not synonymous. I seem to follow sociologist Peter Berger's interpretation of religion: "Religious contents are 'de-objectivated,' that is, deprived of their status as taken for granted, objective reality in consciousness. They become 'subjectivized' [. . .] 'reality' becomes a 'private' affair of individuals" (qtd. in Taylor 227). On the one hand, I fully agree with the notion of religion as a personal and subjective affair that remains the business of the individual alone. Furthermore, I think the equation of subjective and objective realities holds the possibility of great danger and social conflict. Thus, I tend to find comfort in the "hermeneutics of suspicion" of scholars like Nietzsche, Marx, and Freud (Mahaffey Lecture Notes).

On the other hand, I am deeply affected by archetypal theory, influenced heavily by Jung, and relate to religion through the kaleidoscopic lens of *mythopoiesis*, psychologically concerned with images of the unconscious. Religion, if riddled with imposed social stigmas, prejudices, gender hierarchies, or unchecked projections that lead to political spectacle and corruption of the legal system, provokes tension within me. However, religion, if synonymous with a spirituality that aids in one's life journey, is something that not only contributes to my genuine love for mythology and psychology, but falls into the "to each his/her own" category. Somewhere in between these definitions lies my particular brand of atheism and my approach to the God-image.

In *Toward a True Kinship of Faiths,* the Dalai Lama suggests that atheists adhere to a kind of innate humanism: "The secular or nonreligious approach, whereby no religious concepts are evoked but, rather, recognition of the primacy of compassion may be underpinned by common sense, shared common experience, and scientific findings that demonstrate our deep dependence on others' kindness" (109). While I disagree that all religions and non-religions converge in the ideal of compassion and kindness, I do personally subscribe to this statement. I have also traveled to see and have my books signed by a few of the so-called New Atheists, namely Richard Dawkins and Sam Harris, and I can agree that common sense humanism has been a prominent message. However, I disagree with the New Atheists' notion that religion is the number one reason for sexism, racism, and violence. I think that religion is used this way at times, but I also think it is a dangerous framework of externalization and scapegoating to believe that all shadow elements would completely disappear were we to outlaw religion.

I also dislike the New Atheists' approach to feminism within religion, as perfectly summed up by Dawkins in *The God Delusion*: "I suppose that, in the ditzily unreal intersection of theology and feminism, existence might indeed be a less salient attribute than gender" (57). Dawkins not only expresses a condescending attitude toward the important work of female scholarship and biblical hermeneutics, but he demeans the socio-political urgency of re-visioning outdated narratives that so obviously permeate almost every aspect of culture. Dawkins's statement also reveals the most off-putting component of the New Atheist ideology: the implication that those with religious beliefs are unintelligent and irrational. As a mythologist, I am also constantly frustrated with their limited definition of religion, confined as it is to the belief in a Judeo-Christian supernatural deity, without acknowledging the benefits of religion: community, iconography, metaphor, myth, art, ritual, inspiration, charity, and comfort. Yet, I think the New Atheists are entitled to their opinion, and that the Apollonian archetype has its place, too, (providing reason and logic, and scientific discoveries that lead to medical cures and space exploration), so long as it doesn't try to annihilate every other existing archetype.

Turning to more personal and concrete examples of my life vis-à-vis religion is difficult, because for better or for worse, my subjective experiences as a woman and as a minority have impacted my views on the subject. Growing up in what was an overwhelmingly liberal part of Santa Barbara in the 2000s, I was confronted by many racial slurs, death threats, and lynching jokes by those citing their respective religions as justification for hate. My own grandparents refused to attend my parents' mixed-race wedding. Obviously, fundamentalist extremism and the ignorance of a few individuals do not represent an entire tradition, but nevertheless, have been part of my immediate reality. Personally, I am still trying to go deeper within myself to confront my own shadow in regard to these instances, and to enter into the imaginal realm where I can reflect on things like projection and complexes, my own included, that lead to different interpretations of myth or narrative and, thus, to different psycho-social dynamics.

Therefore, when confronting religion, I make distinctions between personal religion and organized religion, between theory and practice, and between literalist and hermeneutic approaches to doctrine. For me, religion, like most things, must be understood on a case-by-case basis, dependent entirely on the individual and his or her relation to the world. I apply this same logic to non-religions. For example, during my brief stint on the Feminist Caucus of the American Humanist Association, I was asked to provide input and to advocate for its new platform on sexuality, which touted the viable and misunderstood vocations of prostitution and pornography for young women. It seems, absurdly, that I have circled back to a suspicion of organized *anything* and find myself moving ever closer to Nietzsche, Kierkegaard, and Luther, in what Taylor describes as "the interiority of the isolated individual" (228).

It is at about this time down the rabbit hole of reflection that I come to fully endorse Jung's sentiment that, "Man's suffering does not derive from his sins but from the maker of his imperfections, the paradoxical God," though, here, I prefer the term God-image (qtd. in Edinger 49). Still, despite my typology as a melancholic introvert, I haven't become a nihilist or a pessimist, or descended into some sort of *materialigion*. Nor have I lost all of those feelings associated with my Beloved of years ago. I am happily awe-inspired by the beauty of the cosmos, by stars and moons, by rivers and mountains, by family and friends, by music and poetry, and by the study of mythology. I would simply classify these things—my God-image—empirically instead of religiously, perhaps as a type of naturalism. On the other hand, I suspect, as Dawkins suggests, that this kind of romantic pantheism is merely just a "sexed-up atheism" (40).

CHAPTER 23

AFTER GOD:
BIRTH OF THE DIVINE ARTIST

Odette Springer

In response to a book sent to him by Pastor Walter Vernet, C. G. Jung wrote about his father's eroding faith: "It was the tragedy of my youth to see my father cracking up before my eyes on the problem of his faith and dying an early death" (qtd. in Edinger 15). As Edward Edinger astutely points out, Jung's experience with his father led him to recognize this rupture as an inner and outer shattering of a two-thousand-year-old Christian dogma (15). This theological unraveling set Jung on a search for a new personal and collective God-Image (Edinger 16). Edinger's analysis of Jung regarding religion thus aligns with my own experiences of spiritual quest. Jung's body of work and, in particular, his autobiography, *Memories, Dreams, Reflections*, speak to this quest, as does his "profound concern with religious questions and with the spiritual aspect of psychology" (Odajnyk 197).

Like Jung's father, the crumbling of an almighty masculine protector shaped my mother's religious reality. I, too, was deeply influenced by her lack of faith in a transcendent power. Instead of searching for a new meaning, the mantra she belabored was, "How could God kill six million Jews?" The incomprehensibility of this question haunted me as I grew up. Swirling about like an unsolvable koan, the Holocaust became the story that contextualized my religious origins. It is not surprising, then, that early on I abandoned my spiritual heritage. Instead, I migrated to Buddhism and Hinduism, which provided a sense of meaning and led me to become part of a movement of very cool people, many of them Jews, beat poets, and alluring mythologists. It was only recently, when I discovered on a Dutch website the list of my 140 family members and the dates of their gassing, that I experienced an unnamable grief. This heartache, which I had cleverly cloaked in meditation, mantras, rituals, Zen calligraphy, tea ceremonies, and tantric and ascetic practices, has made me revisit my motives in keeping Judaism, and, more importantly, Hebrew mythology, at bay.

Perhaps my sense of feeling out of place, disconnected, and lost, is due in part to having discarded the essence of my spiritual inheritance. I can recall only a handful of times when I experienced an authentic sense of relatedness to myself and to the world and every one of those involved participation with Jewish rituals. I recall, in particular, when I fell in love with a Jewish boy, at the Manhattan School of Music, where I was attending the preparatory division. We were both eleven. He had invited me to a seder and I graciously accepted. I had never experienced such a deep sense of connectedness and belonging. Being part of a loving family, practicing a tradition that remembers and honors its history, laughing, praying, singing, and sharing stories, filled me with a sense of profound joy. Tragically, while visiting his family in Israel later that year, he was killed. I never realized how heartbroken I was. It is only recently that I grieved his loss, realizing how out of place I feel in the New Age world where statues of the Buddha and Hindu gods and goddesses are often used as decorative designer props indicating that one is "conscious," or at least on the right side of striving for enlightenment. As a result, my spiritual practice is becoming very private and it meanders and questions.

My attraction to Zen stemmed from a desire to express myself as simply, directly, and authentically as I could. By following my breath, I learned to be with myself, as I am. It was an entry into my interior life. Moreover, Zen provided a father archetype, a powerful, yet stern container for my symbolic life. Of late, however, I've stopped meditating. I am questioning the very symbols that once gave me meaning, as if the death of God has led to the death of all belief systems. Now I am wondering if my attraction to Zen was an unconscious longing for the father—the God—who abandoned me. If so, where and how does the Goddess fit in?

Although Christine Downing points out that "Auschwitz prepared the way for the 'Death of God' and the 'Death of God' in turn helped prepare the way for the 'Rebirth of the Goddess'" (43), this was not the case for me. The mere idea of the Goddess was intimidating; the privileging of the feminine, terrifying. In fact, when I first came to Pacifica, relating to the archetypal Feminine and to the Goddess myths seemed impossible. I, like my mother, had renounced my feminine instincts, just as the culture has denigrated most of them.

In order to return to the Goddess, I had to first examine and then deconstruct the source of my indoctrination. To my great surprise, while approaching the Old Testament, I was confronted by a stark, disturbing realization: the patriarchal interpretation of the Bible was indelibly imprinted on my thinking process. How did this happen? I was raised by atheists and was a self-proclaimed atheist and Buddhist. I could not even move on to Genesis 3 before addressing the problem that arose in Genesis 1 and 2. Where I was tilting the balance— identifying with the male, authoritative voice over the female— demanded an exploration of my bias and prejudice against my own sex. Uncovering that part of my psyche that hated the feminine, did not value it, and was not in partnership with it, horrified me. Yet I also understood that it was natural to gravitate towards men because they held the power that women lacked.

Reading Genesis 1 and 2 over and over, I became aware of how deeply the Bible's masculinist approach weakened Eve's influence as a feminine role model and how powerfully the male-dominated character of scripture shaped my image of women. Even though man and woman are a mutually arising phenomenon in the same way that Yin and Yang are mutually arising in Taoist practice, the male term is consistently privileged over the female. Not only was the story of our physical universe created by a male God, it was written in masculinist language: "And God saw all that *He* had made and found it very good" (Gen 1: 31, emphasis added). So where and in whom are women to trace their roots? Did our roots descend into a male Earth? All the more problematic is Genesis 2, in which God apparently had a change of heart by creating Eve out of Adam's rib: "And the Lord God fashioned the rib that He had taken from the man into a woman" (Gen. 2: 22). In other words, Eve is a male derivative.

I made every attempt to understand God's motives. Could it be that God gave Adam literary primacy because Eve possessed the power to create life, just like God? Was Eve's subordination God's way of leveling the playing field between man and woman? Or was it that God identified with Adam as a male, therefore blaming Eve instead of Adam for eating from the tree of knowledge? Since Eve and God shared the power of giving birth, perhaps God knew that Eve was a threat. What's more, Adam was asleep for Eve's birth. Seen psychologically, he was unconscious of feminine nature. By eating of the tree of knowledge, Eve gave birth to consciousness, yet she is often demonized for doing so. The death of God, therefore, frees us from the literalization of a myth that we have passed on as a religious truth, one that has given rise to the gross inequalities and abuse women have experienced in the West for two thousand years.

I am in the process of a drastic revisioning of a personal and collective Goddess/God-image. I am learning that my sense of estrangement, however disconcerting, is necessary for personal growth. That is because individuation, rather than being a goal, is a cyclical process of self-discovery. My previous life has lost its meaning, and the future holds a promise of the unknown, but I must surrender. I am at a crossroads. Through my course work in mythological studies, I believe I am being empowered to incorporate Jung's creed, *follow your libido wherever it takes you*. This is a terrifying proposition.

Yet, as Mark C. Taylor promises, it is only "on the edge" that theologians make new discoveries. In this way, the seeker, like the artist, walks the razor's edge of the *nekyia*, descending into the unconscious in order to find one's way. Rather than calling myself a feminist, I would prefer to say that I am a lover of the imaginal realm, which transcends the female/male chasm. As an artist, I privilege creativity above all else. I stand with Taylor, who insists that the death of the moral God gives way to the birth of the divine artist. Haven't we always created Goddess and God in our own image anyway?

CHAPTER 24

GOD AS THE PROJECTION OF HUMANITY'S SELF

Dane Styler

> Both Hegel and Christian theology . . . make the same
> error. Both talk about some alien being—about God or
> the absolute—when what they are really talking about is
> humanity, and nothing more. Christian theologians notice all
> of the personal qualities we most dearly admire—ideals like
> goodness, beauty, truthfulness, wisdom, love, steadfastness,
> and strength of character—then proceed to strip them from
> their human owners and project them onto the screen of
> heaven, where they are worshipped—now in a form separate
> from ourselves—under the name of a supernatural being called
> God. (Pals 133)

From my childhood forward into my early adult life, God was always an alien to me. He was this foreign entity, the Other, but this somehow felt wrong, as if just beyond my comprehension I knew that he originated from within. He had been removed and placed outside of myself, and thus the relationship between us was broken. This brokenness was conveniently explained to a pensive, perplexed boy to be the wound caused by sin, and that both faith and a lifetime of atoning good works were needed to heal the rift between God and myself. But God possessed complicated human attributes as well: he was the Father, the Authority, love, vengeful fury, and mercy. He was at once something inhuman yet very human. Silently sitting in the pew with my family in the chapel on Sunday mornings, I struggled with that contradiction of the alien and the familiar existing in one image, one idea.

I was raised in a very conservative Christian home and church community; more specifically, I was raised Mormon—a religion that felt that Christianity didn't already have enough history, doctrine, and theology. I remember sitting in the pews on Sundays, watching the speaker at the pulpit point up to the ceiling, and declare that that was where God lived. The chapel hall ceiling had a lowered middle section that zigzagged toward the front, ending with two slightly recessed light fixtures that lit the pulpit. I imagined that heaven and God rested on the back of a serpent. And yet, I was also told that God lived in my heart, if I was a good boy. I certainly didn't feel his internal presence though, as much as I tried to pretend, in hopes it would just come true. Even as a child, I knew something just didn't sit right with me about God and religion, and the way it changed people's thinking and their behavior. As soon as my mother stopped going to church when I was eleven, I stopped going as well. My father would ground me every Sunday morning and my mother would release me from my prison as soon as his car pulled off the driveway, with my three brothers in tow.

I had a later resurgence of involvement with religion and Christianity in my late teens and early twenties. At one point I was being groomed to be a pastor, though I soon recovered. Another decade later, I find myself reading the passage quoted at the start of this essay, which explains Ludwig Feuerbach's idea that God is a projection of the psyche. The perplexed boy sitting in church on Sundays had finally found the words he had been looking for. God is us looking at ourselves—he is the mirror; it is the anthropomorphism of psychic contents at its finest, projecting the divine elements of the unconscious onto an external image to which we can better relate. God is a human creation, an attempt to understand and give image to the *mysterium tremendum* or numinous that is ineffable. While Feuerbach's ideas influenced Karl Marx and very possibly Friedrich Nietzsche, famous for saying "God is dead," it wasn't until the founding of depth and archetypal psychology that we began to understand clearly that God has always been within, in the realms of the psyche and the mythic imagination.

Why do we seem to need an external God? Why can we not just recognize the divine in everything around us and within us, as it occurs in Eastern traditions? Is it because we feel incomplete unto ourselves, and therefore we desire that father figure to turn to? We want to be loved and have someone to be devoted to, who will take care of us and plan our futures so we don't have to consider our actions today. He is our excuse to neglect our role as caretaker of our home because we think he will clean up our mess so long as we seek forgiveness. More importantly, with a divine and alien God, it is not necessary to carry our own inner, moral code because he provides it for us. The problem is that he is not real, he is not going to save us when we destroy the planet and our race; he is merely a manifestation of those psychic contents culled from the collective unconscious. He is an image created out of fear: our fear of the unknown, of death or chaos, and of meaninglessness. He exists because we want so badly for him to be real.

What is not being realized enough, by enough people in our globalizing community, is that the propagation of the God-image is culturally harmful and an act of destructive nihilism. Since God is alien, he is Other and, thus, we are alienating ourselves *from* ourselves. We are separating part of our psyche, the part that is of divine nature, from ourselves, creating a gap and emptiness within. We fill that hole with all varieties of noises and addictions, including religions and ideologies, for they "are all attempts to create meaning for human beings who, if they had not suffered some sort of primary loss early on, would not need it" (Berman 22). Mark C. Taylor, in his book, *After God*, supports this idea of psychic compensation: "religious experience is supposed to restore momentarily the primal unity that is inevitably lost when consciousness and self-consciousness emerge" (187). But what is worse is that the idea of a personal God creates an opposition and a dividing chasm between the "human and the divine" and "self and world" (Taylor 187). In essence, this monotheistic image of the Christian God stands between us and nature, and it alienates us from our own home. My question becomes less about why we need a God, but what would the world be like without God? Can the world be saved if God is forgotten?

What if God—not the image, but the real deal—actually exists? When asked to consider who or what God might be, I am careful not to say too easily that there is no God or that God is dead. My preference is to choose to recognize that any limiting definition is an error. As something numinous, God would be indefinable; for once you put God in a box, you have lost him.

Recommended Reading

Armstrong, Karen. *Twelve Steps to a Compassionate Life*. New York: Toronto, 2011.

Baring, Ann, and Jules Cashford. *The Myth of the Goddess: Evolution of an Image*. London: Arkana/Penguin, 1991.

Baring, Anne. *The Dream of the Cosmos: A Quest for the Soul*. Dorset, England: Archive Publishing, 2013.

Bstan-'dzin-rgya-mtso, Dalai Lama XIV. *Beyond Religion: Ethics for a Whole World*. Boston: Houghton Mifflin Harcourt, 2011.

—. *Toward a True Kinship of Faiths: How the World's Religions Can Come Together*. New York: Three Rivers Press, 2010.

Campbell, Joseph. *The Hero With a Thousand Faces*. 3rd ed. Novato, CA: New World Library, 2008.

—. *The Inner Reaches of Outer Space: Metaphor as Myth and as Religion*. Novato, CA: New World Library, 2012.

Compte-Sponville, Andre. *The Little Book of Atheist Spirituality*. New York: Penguin, 2006.

*Corbett, Lionel. *Psyche and the Sacred: Spirituality Beyond Religion*. New Orleans: Spring Journal Books, 2007.

Dawkins, Richard. *The God Delusion*. Boston: Mariner, 2006.

Dennett, Daniel C. *Breaking the Spell: Religion as a Natural Phenomenon*. New York: Penguin, 2006.

De Botton, Alain. *Religion for Atheists*. New York: Pantheon, 2012.

*Downing, Christine. *The Goddess: Mythological Images of the Feminine*. Lincoln, NE: Authors Choice Press, 2007.

—. *Gods In Our Midst: Mythological Images of the Masculine: A Woman's View*. New York: Crossroad, 1993.

Edinger, Edward F. *The Creation of Consciousness: Jung's Myth for Modern Man*. Inner City Books, 1984.

—. *Ego and Archetype: Individuation and the Religious Function of the Psyche*. Boston: Shambhala, 1992.

—. *The New God Image: A Study of Jung's Key Letters Concerning the Evolution of the Western God-Image*. Ed. Dianne D. Cordic and Charles Yates. Wilmette, IL: Chiron Publications, 1996.

Freud, Sigmund. *The Future of an Illusion*. New York: W. W. Norton & Co., 1961.

Gross, Rita M. *Feminism and Religion*. Boston: Beacon, 1996.

Hick, John. *An Interpretation of Religion: Human Responses to the Transcendent*. 2nd ed. New Haven: Yale UP, 2005.

—. *God Has Many Names*. Philadelphia: Westminster John Knox, 1982.

Hillman, James. *Insearch: Psychology and Religion*. 2nd ed. Woodstock, CT: Spring Publications, 1994.

James, William. *The Varieties of Religious Experience*. New York: Penguin Books, 1982.

Jung, C. G. *Answer to Job.* Trans. R. F. C. Hull. Fiftieth-anniversary ed. Princeton: Princeton UP, 1973. Print.

—. *Memories, Dreams, Reflections.* Ed. Aniela Jaffé. New York: Vintage Books, 1963.

—. *The Red Book: Liber Novus. A Reader's Edition.* Ed. Sonu Shamdasani. New York: W. W. Norton & Co., 2009.

*Le Grice, Keiron. *The Rebirth of the Hero: Mythology as a Guide to Spiritual Transformation.* London: Musewell Hill Press, 2013.

Marx, Karl, and Friedrich Engels. *Karl Marx and Friedrich Engels on Religion.* New York: Schoken Books, 1964.

Nietzsche, Friedrich. *Beyond Good and Evil: Prelude to a Philosophy of the Future.* Trans. Walter Kaufmann. New York: Vintage Books, 1966. Print.

—. *The Gay Science, with a Prelude of Rhymes and an Appendix of Songs.* Trans. Walter Kaufman. New York: Random House, 1974. Print.

Nhat, Hanh. *Going Home: Jesus and Buddha as Brothers.* New York: Riverhead Books, 1999.

—. *Living Buddha, Living Christ.* New York: Riverhead Books, 1995.

*Odajnyk, V. Walter *Gathering the Light: A Jungian View of Meditation.* Carmel, CA: Fisher King Press, 2011.

*Paris, Ginette. *Pagan Grace: Dionysos, Hermes, and Goddess Memory in Daily Life.* Woodstock, CT: Spring Publications, 1998.

—. *Pagan Meditations: The Worlds of Aphrodite, Artemis, and Hestia.* Woodstock, CT: Spring Publications, 1998.

*Slattery, Dennis P. *Grace in the Desert: Awakening to the Gifts of Monastic Life*. San Francisco: Jossey-Bass, 2004.

—. *Riting Myth, Mythic Writing: Plotting Your Personal Story*. Carmel, CA: Fisher King Press, 2012.

*Smith, Evans Lansing. *Sacred Mysteries: Myths About Couples in Quest*. Nevada City, CA. Blue Dophin Publishing, 2003.

Smith, Huston. *Tales of Wonder: Adventures Chasing the Divine*. New York: HarperOne, 2009.

—. *Why Religion Matters: The Fate of the Human Spirit in an Age of Disbelief*. New York: HarperSanFrancisco, 2001.

Taylor, Mark C. *After God*. Chicago: U of Chicago P, 2007. Print.

Vaughan-Lee, Llewellyn. *The Return of the Feminine & the World Soul*. Point Reyes, CA: The Golden Sufi Center, 2009.

Vivekananda, Swami. *Pathways to Joy: The Master Vivekananda on the Four Yoga Paths to God*. Ed. Dave De Luca. Makawo, HI: Inner Ocean Publishing, 2003.

Wilber, Ken. *Integral Spirituality: A Startling New Role for Religion in the Modern and Postmodern World*. Boston: Integral Books, 2006. Print.

*Woodman, Marion. *Leaving My Father's House: A Journey to Conscious Femininity*. Boston: Shambhala, 1993. Print.

*Woodman, Marion, and Elinor Dickson. *Dancing in the Flames: The Dark Goddess in the Transformation of Consciousness*. Boston: Shambhala, 1996.

*Books by professors and associates at Pacifica Graduate Institute

WORKS CITED

Altizer, Thomas J. J. *The Gospel of Christian Atheism*. Philadelphia: Westminster Press, 1966. Print.

Armstrong, Karen. "My Wish: The Charter of Compassion." February 2008. TED.com. Web. 13 Aug. 2012.

—. *Twelve Steps to a Compassionate Life*. New York: Alfred A. Knopf, 2011. Print.

Berger, Peter L. *The Heretical Imperative: Contemporary Possibilities of Religious Affirmation*. New York: Anchor Press/Doubleday, 1980. Print.

—. *The Sacred Canopy: Elements of a Sociological Theory of Religion*. New York: Anchor Books, 1990. Print.

Berman, Morris. *Coming to Our Senses: Body and Spirit in the Hidden History of the West*. New York: Bantam Books, 1990. Print.

Blake, William. *The Complete Poetry and Prose of William Blake*. Ed. David V. Erdman. New York: Anchor, 1988. Print.

Boom, Corrie Ten, and Sherrill, Elizabeth and John. *The Hiding Place*. 4th ed. Peabody, MA: Hendrickson Publishing, 2012. Print.

Briggs, Katharine C., and Isabel Briggs Myers. *Myers-Briggs Type Indicator: Form G-Self Scorable Question Booklet*. Palo Alto, CA: Consulting Psychologists Press, 1988. Print.

Bstan-'dzin-rgya-mtso, Dalai Lama XIV. *Beyond Religion: Ethics for a Whole World.* Boston: Houghton Mifflin Harcourt, 2011. Print.

—. *Toward a True Kinship of Faiths: How the World's Religions Can Come Together.* New York: Three Rivers Press, 2010. Print.

Bultmann, Rudolf. *Jesus Christ and Mythology.* New York: Charles Scribner's Sons, 1958.

Campbell, Joseph. *The Hero's Journey: Joseph Campbell on His Life and Work.* Ed. Phil Cousineau. Novato, CA: New World Library, 2003. Print.

—. *The Inner Reaches of Outer Space: Metaphor as Myth and as Religion.* Novato, CA: New World Library, 1986. Print.

—. *Pathways to Bliss: Mythology and Personal Transformation.* Ed. David Kudler. Novato, CA: New World Library, 2004. Print.

Cowan, Louise. *Texas Myths.* Ed. Robert F. Connor. College Station: Texas A & M UP, 1984. 1-22. Print.

Daniélou, Alain. *Shiva and Dionysus.* Trans. K.F. Hurry. Southampton: The Camelot Press Ltd., 1982. Print.

Daniels, David, and Virginia Price. *The Essential Enneagram: The Definitive Personality Test and Self-Discovery Guide.* San Francisco: Harper, 2000. Print.

Dawkins, Richard. *The God Delusion.* Boston: Mariner, 2006. Print.

De Botton, Alain. "Atheism 2.0." July 2011. TED.com. Web. 3 June 2013.

Downing, Christine. *The Luxury of Afterwards.* Lincoln, NE: iUniverse, 2004. Print.

Dyer, Donald R. *Jung's Thoughts on God: Religious Depths of the Psyche.* York Beach, ME: Nicolas-Hays, 2000. Print.

Easwaran, Eknath. *The Bhagavad Gita.* New York: Vintage Spiritual Classics, 2000.

Edinger, Edward. *The New God Image: A Study of Jung's Key Letters Concerning the Evolution of the Western God-Image.* Ed. Dianne D. Cordic and Charles Yates. Wilmette, IL: Chiron Publications, 1996. Print.

Franz, Marie-Louise von. "The Process of Individuation." *Man and His Symbols.* Ed. C. G. Jung and Marie-Louise von Franz. London: Aldus Books, 1964. 158-229. Print.

Gilligan, Carol. *In a Different Voice: Psychological Theory and Women's Development.* Cambridge: Harvard UP, 1993.

Golas, Thadeus. *The Lazy Man's Guide to Enlightenment.* Salt Lake City: Gibbs Smith Publisher, 1971. Print.

The Gospel of Thomas: The Hidden Sayings of Jesus. Trans. Marvin Meyer. San Francisco: Harper San Francisco, 1992. Print.

Hammond, Phillip E. Introduction. *The Sacred in a Secular Age: Towards Revision in the Scientific Study of Religion.* Ed. Phillip E. Hammond, ed. Berkeley: U of California P, 1985. 1-6. Print.

Heidegger, Martin. *Basic Writings.* Ed. David Farrell Krell. San Francisco, CA: Harper & Row, 1977. Print.

Heinlein, Robert. *Time Enough for Love.* New York, NY. Ace Publishing. 1973. Print.

Hillman, James. *Re-Visioning Psychology.* New York: Harper Collins, 1975.

Howell, Alice O. *Jungian Symbolism in Astrology: Letters from an Astrologer*. Wheaton, IL: Theosophical Publishing House, 1987. Print.

Jacobi, Jolande. *Complex, Archetype and Symbol in the Psychology of C.G. Jung*. Princeton: Princeton UP, 1971. Print.

James, William. *The Varieties of Religious Experience*. New York: Penguin Books, 1982. Print.

Jung, C. G. *Aion: Researches into the Phenomenology of the Self*. Trans. R. F. C. Hull. 2nd ed. Princeton: Princeton UP, 1969. Print.

—. *Answer to Job*. Trans. R. F. C. Hull. Fiftieth-anniversary ed. Princeton: Princeton UP, 1973. Print.

—. *The Collected Works of C. G. Jung*. Trans. R. F. C. Hull. Vol. 9i. Princeton: Princeton UP, 1990. Print.

—. "General Aspects of Dream Psychology." Trans. R. F. C. Hull. *The Collected Works of C. G.* Jung. Vol. 8. Princeton: Princeton UP, 1959. 237-280. Print.

—. *Letters*. Vol. 2. Eds. Gerhard Adler and Aniela Jaffé. Princeton: Princeton UP, 1975.

—. *Memories, Dreams, Reflections*. Ed. Aniela Jaffe. Trans. Richard and Clara Winston. New York: Vintage Books, 1963. Print.

—. "The Practical Use of Dream Analysis." The *Collected Works of C. G. Jung*. Vol. 16: Trans. R.F.C. Hull. London. Routledge and Kegan Paul, 1954. 139-161. Print.

—. *The Red Book: Liber Novus*. Ed. Sonu Shamdasani. Trans. Mark Kyburz, John Peck, and Sonu Shamdasani. New York: W. W. Norton & Co., 2009. Print.

Kuttner, Fred, *Quantum Enigma*. New York: Oxford University Press, 2006

Lao Tzu. *Tao Te Ching: Annotated & Explained*. Trans. Derek Lin. Web: SkyLight Paths, 2006. Web.

Le Grice, Keiron. *The Archetypal Cosmos: Rediscovering the Gods in Myth, Science and Astrology*. Edinburgh: Floris Books, 2010. Print.

Mahaffey, Patrick. Course on the God Complex. Pacifica Graduate Institute. Lecture Notes. 21 May 2013. Lecture.

Marion Woodman: Dancing in the Flames. Dir. Adam Geydon Reid. Perf. Marion Woodman, Andrew Harvey, Ross Woodman. Caprivision/Marion Woodman Foundation, 2009. DVD.

McFarlane, Thomas J., ed. *Einstein and Buddha: The Parallel Sayings*. Berkeley, CA: Seastone, 2002.

Merleau-Ponty, Maurice. *Phenomenology of Perception*. Trans. Donald A. Landes. New York: Routledge, 1945.

Myers, Isabel Briggs and Peter B. Briggs. *Gifts Differing*. Palo Alto, CA: Consulting Psychologist's Press, 1980.

Nietzsche, Friedrich. *Beyond Good and Evil: Prelude to a Philosophy of the Future*. Trans. Walter Kaufmann. New York: Vintage Books, 1966. Print.

—. *The Gay Science, with a Prelude of Rhymes and an Appendix of Songs*. Trans. Walter Kaufman. New York: Random House, 1974. Print.

Odajnyk, V. Walter *Archetype and Character: Eros and Matter Personality Types*. New York: Palgrave Macmillan, 2012. Print.

Osborne, Joan, perf. "One of Us." By Eric Bazilian. *Relish*. Philadelphia: Blue Gorilla/Mercury, 1995. LP.

Pals, Daniel L. *Eight Theories of Religion.* 2ⁿᵈ ed. New York: Oxford UP, 2006.

Panikkar, Raimundo. *The Silence of God: The Answer of the Buddha.* Trans. Robert R. Barr. Maryknoll, NY: Orbis Books, 1990. Print.

Plaskow, Judith, and Carol P. Christ, eds. *Weaving the Visions: New Patterns in Feminist Spirituality.* San Francisco: Harper & Row, 1989. Print.

Plato. *The Symposium and the Phaedrus: Plato's Erotic Dialogues.* Trans. William S. Cobb. Albany, NY: State University of New York, 1993. Print.

Pohren, D.E. *The Art of Flamenco.* Seville: Society of Spanish Studies, 1972. Print

Raff, Jeff. *Jung and the Alchemical Imagination.* Berwick, ME: Nicolas-Hayes, 2000. Print.

Samuels, Andrew, and Bani Shorter and Fred Plaut. *A Critical Dictionary of Jungian Analysis.* London and New York: Routledge, 1986. Print.

Schleiermacher, Friedrich. *On Religion: Speeches to its Cultured Despisers.* Trans. John Oman. New York: Harper & Row, 1958. Print.

Smith, Curtis. *Jung's Quest for Wholeness: A Religious and Historical Perspective.* Albany: State U of New York P, 1990. Print.

Smith, Wilfred Cantwell. *Towards a World Theology: Faith and the Comparative History of Religions.* Philadelphia: Westminter Press, 1981. Print.

Starhawk. *Truth or Dare: Encounters with Power, Authority, and Mystery.* San Francisco: Harper & Row, 1987. Print.

Tarnas, Richard. *Jung, Cosmology, and the Transformation of the Modern Self.* Santa Barbara, CA. Depth Video, 2006. DVD.

Taylor, Mark C. *After God.* Chicago: U of Chicago P, 2007. Print.

Vaughan-Lee, Llewellyn. *The Return of the Feminine & the World Soul: A Collection of Writings and Transcribed Talks.* Inverness, CA: Golden Sufi Center, 2009. Print.

Wennemyr, Susan E. *Theology After Modernity,* Chicago: U of Chicago, 1995. Print.

Wilber, Ken. *Integral Spirituality: A Startling New Role for Religion in the Modern and Posmodern World.* Boston: Integral Books, 2006. Print.

Woodman, Marion. *Coming Home to Myself: Reflections on Nurturing A Woman's Body and Soul.* Berkeley, CA: Conari Press, 1998. Print.

—. *Leaving My Father's House: A Journey to Conscious Femininity.* Boston: Shambhala, 1993. Print.

—. *The Pregnant Virgin: A Process of Psychological Transformation.* Toronto, Canada: Inner City, 1985. Print.

LIST OF CONTRIBUTORS

Patrick J. Mahaffey, Ph.D., is a professor and associate chair of the Mythological Studies Program at Pacifica Graduate Institute, which he chaired for eighteen years. His teaching and research focus on Hindu and Buddhist traditions, comparative philosophy of religion, and contemplative practices. He has practiced Hindu and Buddhist forms of meditation for forty years, has participated in retreats at ashrams in India and Australia, and has lectured at the Parliament of World Religions in Melbourne. His publications include essays on C. G. Jung and Hindu yoga traditions, Hindu mythos, Buddhist mythos, and religious pluralism.

Christine Downing, Ph.D., is a professor in the Mythological Studies Program at Pacifica Graduate Institute and Professor Emeritus of Religious Studies at San Diego State University. She is the author of numerous books and scholarly articles on religion, mythology, literature, depth psychology, and gender studies. Among her most influential books are: *The Goddess: Mythological Images of the Feminine*; *Myths and Mysteries of Same-Self Love*; *Psyche's Sisters*; *Women's Mysteries*; and *The Long Journey Home: Revisioning the Myth of Demeter and Persephone for Our Time*.

Julia Berg, native of Kansas, married mother of two married daughters and grandmother of six, holds a B.M., a B.ME., an M.ME. in Music, and an M.A. in Counseling Psychology. She has performed as a pianist, concert and church organist, and taught vocal music, music performance, and theory for many years. In addition, she has published works including educational multi-media keyboard music programs and many articles on performance and music education in MTAC journals. She is the co-author of two books: *The Parent's Medical*

Manual and *The Parent's Guide To Child Raising*. Her second career in psychotherapy involved the founding and running of a non-profit organization that offers grief counseling, for which she wrote the charter and the training handbook. Her doctoral research examines the issues of transsexuals in marital relationships.

Susan Chaney, a native of Montana, currently lives in Southern California. She holds a B.A. in Psychology and Spirituality from Antioch University, Seattle. Her work has been published in *Between*, the literary journal of Pacifica Graduate Institute. Susan is a teacher and cultural mythologist who focuses on the merging of body, mind, and soul. Her dissertation focuses on the integration of somatic, psychological, and spiritual being as the goal of individual consciousness.

Alexandra Dragin holds a B.A. in Journalism from Columbia College Chicago and an M.A. in English Language and Literature from DePaul University. She is currently a full-time faculty member in the English department at Triton College, a large community college located just west of Chicago, where she teaches developmental reading, composition, and literature courses. She currently resides with her husband, Aleksandar Dragin, in Oak Park, Illinois. Her dissertation considers the connection between erotic and spiritual love in myth and literature.

Darlene (Maggie) Dowdy holds a B.A. in Interdisciplinary Studies from Emmanuel College and an M.A. in English from Boston College. She has contributed poetry and a short story to *Between*, the literary journal of Pacifica Graduate Institute. Maggie enjoys the creative exchange of ideas and loves a good story. An advocate of literacy, she has volunteered in programs committed to the development of English as a second language. Maggie resides in Massachusetts where she is actively engaged in both the creative aspects and the fundamental operations of an industrial rubber company.

Jacqueline Fry is the mother of three children and six grandchildren. Originally from Austin, Texas, she presently resides in Kansas where she raises German Shepherds and Shih Tzu dogs. Jacqueline has worked at Hutchinson Community College for five years where she teaches a variety of courses including World Religions, Ethics, and Philosophy. She has an A.A. in Communication and Theater from Carl Albert Junior College, a B.A. in Religion and Philosophy from Sterling College, and an M.A. in Christian History from Iliff School of Theology.

Daniel Gurska, a Minnesota native, received his B.A. in Humanities from Sierra Nevada College, Lake Tahoe, with a concentration in psychology. Daniel is aspiring to be a professor in the Humanities and is currently residing in the Santa Barbara area. His current research involves Genesis, Midrash, and Thomas Mann's *Joseph and His Brothers*.

Robert Guyker, Jr., holds a B.F.A. in Painting and Printmaking from Virginia Commonwealth University. He is an instructor at Palos Verdes Art Center and has made presentations on mythology, mythopoetics, and play in digital media at regional and national academic conferences.

Timothy Hall was born in Wyoming and was reputedly raised on venison that his father shot with a bow. Later he lived in a 1948 two-and-a-half ton Chevrolet truck with a wood-burning stove while getting a B.A. in Philosophy from the University of California, Santa Barbara. Under the influence of phenomenology, he came to the realization that all decisions are an art form and that more training in academic philosophy was simply bad art. He subsequently became a nationally recognized glassblower, taught glassblowing, philosophy, and remedial mathematics at Santa Barbara Community College for over thirty years, and traveled extensively. He is writing a dissertation entitled *Iconopoeisis and Reification: Twin Engines in Imagining the World*.

April Heaslip is an educator and mythologist based in southern Vermont. Holding an M.A in Social Ecology from Goddard College and a B.A. in Psychology and Women's Studies from West Chester University, her published work has appeared in the online journal *Depth Insights*, with an upcoming article in *Sage Woman*. Teaching for twenty-six years, primarily in the fields of Gender Studies and Human Ecology, led her to dissertation research that examines the resurgence of Magdalene mythology and its eco-feminist gifts. She is the founder of the Inside-Out-Stitute and practices yoga, *bricolage*, and cultural animation.

James E. Heaton holds a B.A. in English and Philosophy from The College of Santa Fe. His doctoral research focuses on Chinese culture and myth, with an emphasis on divination and esoteric philosophy. His experience with Chinese mythology includes two years living in Beijing, and his involvement with an intercultural marriage and his wife's extended family. He currently resides in southern New Mexico with his wife and daughter.

Gabriel Hilmar grew up in Minnesota and completed a B.A. in Spanish language and culture at the University of Minnesota. As a musician and poet, Gabriel has taught music, dance, and poetry in K-12 schools in Minnesota. He plays guitar, harp, and wooden flute. He is recorded on *Farruca's Dream*, a compact disc of original compositions based upon medieval Celtic and Spanish music. Gabriel is currently writing his dissertation on the Norse God Odin's individual growth from warrior to God of poetry and magic.

Laurie Larsen earned a B.F.A. from California College of the Arts and an M.F.A. from Yale University. After many years pursuing her passion for nurturing creative expression, in herself and others, including her magnificent children, she embarked on an extensive exploration of myth-making in world cultures past, present and future. She lives in the sundrenched lands of the southwest, pondering, researching, writing, painting and reveling in life.

Lynlee Lyckberg holds a B.A. in Studio Art and Art History from California State University, East Bay, and an M.F.A. in Arts and Consciousness, with a concentration in painting from John F. Kennedy University. Lynlee studied Traditional Chinese Arts and Healing at the University of Hangzhou, and has a deep interest in Tibetan Buddhism. She has paintings in the permanent collection of two universities, and has taught art at both the high school and the college level. Her doctoral dissertation focuses on the necessity of artistic expression as a transformational practice in both the individual and the collective psyche.

Clara Oropeza is a native Spanish speaker and holds both baccalaureate and master's degrees in English Literature, with an emphasis on Literature from Latin America, from California State University, Los Angeles. She is an Assistant Professor at Santa Barbara City College where she teaches composition and literature courses. Her work has been published in *Sagewoman*, *Inside English*, and *Journal of Mythological Studies*. Clara lives, plays and writes in Santa Barbara with her husband, Mark Wanek, and their sweet terrier mix, Emma Zunz.

Raised in Crystal City, Texas, Daniel Ortiz has taught English and history to junior high, high school, and community college students for ten years in Texas and California. He earned a B.A. in English, with a minor in history, from Sul Ross State University Rio Grande College in Uvalde, Texas. His dissertation research concerns Sigmund Freud's theory of the death instinct and its role in contemporary America.

Emmanuelle Patrice is a native of Texas. She holds a B.A. in Fashion Design and an M.A. in Film and Literature Studies from California State University Los Angeles.

April F. M. Rasmussen holds a B.A. in Classical Studies and an M.A. in Education. For the past six years, she has taught courses in language arts and humanities in California public schools. She also collaborated with artist Andrew Winegarner on *Gilgamesh: A Graphic Novel*, as a co-author and consultant. Her dissertation focuses on the mythological dimensions of domesticity, a topic near and dear to her as the mother of a vivacious toddler.

Rachel Shakti Redding, Yoga Worldreach Seva School Founding Director and Certified Yoga Therapist, has been teaching Inner Power Yoga® since 2000. She has traveled extensively throughout the world, gaining insight, experience, and inspiration, and bringing yoga and hope to people from all walks of life.

John Redmond grew up in Southern California and holds a B.A. in Religious Studies from the University of Hawaii at Manoa. While in Hawaii, he tutored student athletes in the sciences and humanities and served as a mentor to those facing academic probation. He is one of six children raised by his British ex-Catholic parents in a household where the primary religious fervor revolved around Liverpool Football Club. John's dissertation examines the latest in theoretical physics from a psychological and mythic perspective. He currently resides in Portland, Oregon, with his two cats.

Haydeé Rovirosa was born in Mexico City. She holds a B.A. in Art History and an M.A. in Museum Studies from Universidad Iberoamericana, México. After many years in the art world as curator, art-critic, and sponsor of artists, she decided to become a student again and enrolled in the doctoral program in Mythological Studies at Pacifica Graduate Institute. Her dissertation explores the relationship between ecological consciousness and contemporary art.

Angela Sells, a California native, holds a B.A. in English Literature from the University of California, Santa Barbara. She is a domestic violence prevention educator and currently lectures at Santa Barbara City College's Center for Lifelong Learning in the fields of mythology and literature.

Odette Springer is classically trained in music and graduated from the Manhattan School of Music with a B.A. in Piano. She has been a singer, songwriter, and composer for more than twenty-five films. Odette's feature documentary about Hollywood's B-Movie industry premiered at the Sundance Film Festival and was nominated for the Grand Jury Prize. She has published in *Between*, a literary journal, and the *Mythological Studies Journal*, peer-reviewed publications of Pacifica Graduate Institute.

Dane Styler received a B.A. in English Literature from George Mason University. He is a journalist, playwright, screenwriter, author, and teacher. His dissertation research explores the new developing mythology of homosexuality in American culture.

Elizabeth Wolterink holds a B.A. in Anthropology with a minor in Cinema from SUNY Binghamton. She lives in Traverse City, Michigan, where she is an educator in the Episcopal Church and engages young people in personal development through wilderness camping and martial arts. Elizabeth has also provided services as a mythological and martial arts consultant for the Shakespeare Festival at Interlochen Center for the Arts, and as a freelance film consultant. Her doctoral research involves a cross-cultural exploration of the religious, psychological, and cultural meanings of the feminine journey to the underworld.

INDEX